CHILDREN'S OLD TESTAMENT
BIBLE STORIES

FEATURING Coptic ILLUSTRATIONS

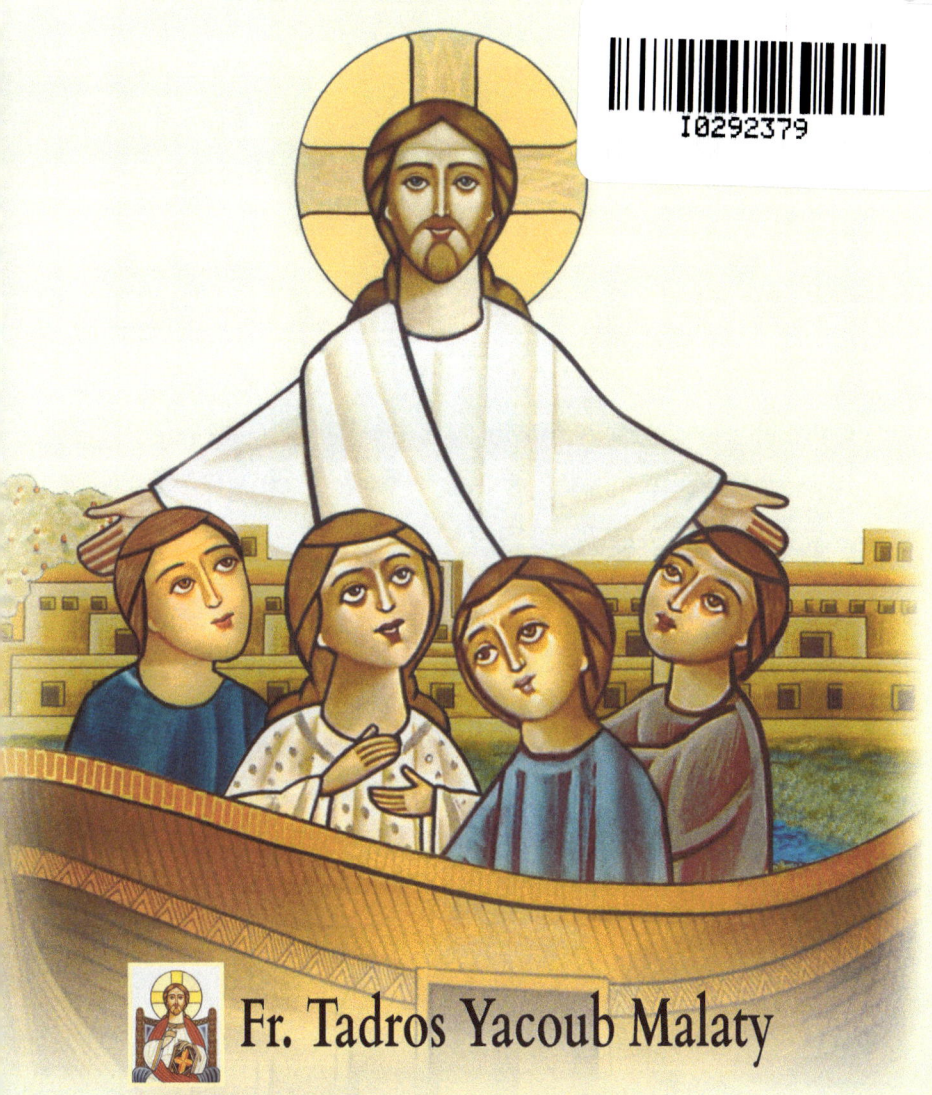

Fr. Tadros Yacoub Malaty

Children's Old Testament Bible Stories, Featuring Coptic Illustrations

Copyright © 2016 by Fr. Tadros Yacoub Malaty

Illustrations by Tasony Sawsan

All rights reserved.

Designed & Published by:
St. Mary & St. Moses Abbey Press
101 S. Vista Dr., Sandia, TX 78383
stmabbeypress.com

Library of Congress Control Number: 2016962274

Children's Old Testament
Bible Stories

Featuring Coptic Illustrations

I am Moses the Prophet

Welcome, dear child, I am Moses the Prophet.

The Lord asked me to rescue my people—the Israelites, from slavery in Egypt. They were suffering under the reign of Pharaoh, the king of Egypt, who forced them to fire clay to make bricks.

My Lord also helped me write the first five books of the Holy Bible, through the guidance of the Holy Spirit. These books are called Genesis, Exodus, Leviticus, Numbers, and Deuteronomy. Some people call them the "Five books of Moses" or the "Torah."

These books are written to teach everyone about God's great love for them. They also show us the joyful life we will live when we obey God and follow Him and what happens when we do not listen to God.

The first book I wrote was the Book of Genesis. In Genesis, God wants to explain how the world in which we live began. He also wants us to read about those who lived a long time ago so that we can learn from their experiences.

In Exodus you can read about how I fasted for 40 days and how the Lord appeared to me and gave me the Ten Commandments.

I will see you once again, God willing, to tell you all about the Lord who loves me and loves you. He loves everyone and wants us all to enjoy heaven, which He has prepared for us.

God Spoke and Made Every Beautiful Thing
～ Genesis 1 ～

Have you heard about the angels and the heavenly creatures? Have you seen the sun that shines during the day, the moon and the stars at night, your family and friends? Have you seen the animals of the land and the birds in the sky?

A very long time ago, there was no sun or moon, nor were there any people, neither young nor old. Everything was dark. God spoke, and when He spoke, He created the sun that shines during the day and the moon and stars that glow by night.

God loved man, even before He created him. In the beginning, there was no light for man to see; there were no humans or animals.

On the first day, God said, "Let there be light," and indeed there was light.

On the second day, God created the firmament to divide the waters and called it "heaven."

On the third day, God gathered the waters together and dry land appeared. God then created the plants.

On the fourth day, God created the sun to give us light and warmth. He also created the moon and the stars to shine in the sky at night.

On the fifth day, God filled the sea with fish and filled the sky with singing birds.

On the sixth day, God created all kinds of animals. He also created Adam, the first man on earth. Everything was so beautiful and that is why God decided to bless the seventh day.

Prayer: Thank you, Lord, for creating this beautiful and wonderful world for me.

The King and Queen in the Castle
Genesis 1–2

Hello, I am Adam. The Lord created a beautiful garden, "the garden of Eden," in which I could live. In this garden, I felt like I was a king living in my castle. I was so happy. God created the world for me and asked me to work in the garden. He asked me to name all the animals, birds, and plants.

God said to me: "Enjoy the garden and all of its trees." Then, He pointed to one tree and said to me, "Do not eat of this tree."

I loved the garden, animals, birds, trees, and flowers, but I was lonely. I needed someone like me that I could love and with whom I could talk. God decided to create a woman called Eve. She became my wife and we were very happy, thanking and praising God. Whenever we heard God walking in the garden, we would walk and talk with Him and He would talk with us.

Prayer: Thank you, Lord, for creating Adam and Eve and for granting them wisdom. Thank you for giving them a mind to think and the freedom to choose.

The Snake Lies to Eve
Genesis 3

Welcome back. This is Adam again. One day, a sneaky snake came to my wife, Eve, and whispered in her ear saying, "Why don't you eat the fruit of this tree?" Eve answered and said to the snake, "We may eat the fruit of every tree in the garden except for the tree of the knowledge of good and evil, because God said that if we eat of it, we will die."

The snake said, "The fruit of this tree is delicious; do not listen to what God says, for whoever eats of the tree will be like God knowing good and evil." Eve believed the snake and picked the fruit and ate it. Then, she offered some to me and I ate it too. Immediately, we were so afraid. We hid from God. We did not know how to meet or talk to Him. We did not listen to God and that is why He took us outside the beautiful garden where we lived. What a sad day!

We became ashamed of being naked, but God did not leave us naked. He made us tunics from animal's skin and He promised us that He would send us a Savior, the Lord Jesus Himself. We could not return to the garden of Eden after that because an angel was guarding it with a sword of fire.

Prayer: Thank you, Lord, because You did not leave us, but You came to us and made us Your children, so that we may live with You in Heaven.

Abel
Genesis 4

I am Abel. I am Adam and Eve's son. I have an older brother. His name is Cain. I loved God with all my heart and always obeyed His words. I was always kind to my parents and brother. As for Cain, sadly, he often did things that were mean and vicious.

Our parents taught us to give offerings to God. I gladly offered the firstborn of my flock. Cain offered fruit from his farm to God. The Lord gladly accepted my offerings because I gave them with a loving heart, but He did not accept my brother's offering, because he gave them without love.

God loved my brother so much and warned him about the evil in his heart. One day, while I was talking with Cain in the field, he grew very angry with me and he killed me. He thought that God and our parents did not see him. This sin grieved God as well as my parents.

God did not leave my brother Cain because He loves everyone, even sinners. He wanted to start a conversation with him, so He asked him about me saying, "Where is Abel, your brother?"

Cain thought that God loved me more than He loved him. He believed that this love was the reason why He accepted my offering and was now asking where I was. Cain could not bear to hear my name because he hated me. Therefore, he answered God, saying, "Am I my brother's keeper?"

Exercise: Try to bring joy to God's heart by keeping His commandments and by loving your siblings. Ask God for His help with this.

The Sons of God and the Daughters of Men
⚘ Genesis 6 ⚘

God wanted to make Adam and Eve happy after the death of their son, Abel, so He gave them another son named, Seth. Seth was a praying and loving man.

Seth had godly children who were called, the "sons of God." As for Seth's brother, Cain, his children's hearts were turned away from God.

Seth's righteous descendants married Cain's descendants and were influenced by them. Cain's descendants were very vicious, even the women, and they taught Seth's sons violence and hatred.

God was sorry that the wickedness of man had increased on the earth. He said, "I will wipe out mankind, whom I have created, from the face of the earth—men and animals, and creatures that move along the ground, and the birds of the air, for I am grieved that I have made them." However, there was one man who was different. This man's name was Noah. God liked what He saw in Noah.

Noah walked with God. He had three sons: Shem, Ham, and Japheth. In God's eyes, the earth was filled with violence, so He wanted to end the violence leaving only Noah and his family to live on the earth.

Question: If the earth is filled with men who do not follow God, does God ever forget the righteous man?

God Protects Me
Genesis 6–9

Hello, my name is Noah. Do you know my story?

God spoke to me saying: "People have filled the earth with wickedness; I will send a flood so that everything will drown and the world will be clean again."

God told me to build an ark, which is like a big ship, and make it one and a half times the length and two times the width of a football field.

I listened to what God said and built the ark with my three sons who helped me make it on the ground. The ark consisted of three floors. As we were building, my friends would make fun of me and ask me, "Why are you building a huge ship on the ground when there is no sea close-by?" I continued to build and build until the ark was ready.

God said to me, "Take your family and two of every kind of animal and bird with you." My family and I entered the ark and God shut the door behind us so the water would not get inside.

It started to rain and rain and rain for 40 days and 40 nights and the underground springs were overflowing from beneath. The ark floated on the surface of the water for 150 days, and no harm came to any person or creature inside the ark.

God remembered me and my family and all the animals and caused a wind to blow making the flood go down.

The rain stopped falling from the sky and the underground springs were closed. I sent a dove outside and it flew back to me, as it did not find any dry land. I sent the dove again and this time it came back with a green olive leaf in its beak. I knew then that the dove had found dry land. The ark landed on top of a mountain in Armenia.

As God saved Noah and His family inside the ark, He will protect us inside the church.

A Rainbow in the Sky
Genesis 8–9

It is me again, Noah.

What are these beautiful colors in the sky?

It is a rainbow!

When we came out from the ark, I built an altar for the Lord and presented a thanksgiving offering to Him for keeping us safe.

Our Lord rejoiced over my thankful heart and He presented me with the promise that whenever the rainbow appears in the sky, it will be a sign of the promise He made—that He will never drown the whole earth with a flood ever again.

God rewards those who listen to Him no matter how few in number they are and He disciplines people on earth because He wants them to grow closer to Him.

A verse from the Holy Bible:

"And Noah did according to all that the LORD commanded him" (Genesis 7:5).

Question: When it rains heavily, a rainbow appears. What does this mean?

The Great Tower
Genesis 11

It did not take long before Noah's sons increased and spread all over the earth, as one place was not large enough for them.

They agreed to make bricks and bake them instead of stones and to use asphalt for mortar. They thought to use the baked bricks and the asphalt to build a city and a great tower to reach the heavens so that they would become famous and be able to climb up the tower whenever God wants to discipline them with a flood.

God was not pleased with this work and He did not allow them to continue building the tower. God made every family speak in a different language so they could not understand what the others were saying. Therefore, they were unable to work together to finish building the city.

The city was called Babel, because God confused their language.

Shem's sons spread across Asia and from them came forth the Israelites (the people of God). Ham's sons settled in Africa. As for Japheth's sons, they crossed over into Europe.

A Long Journey
ᐳ Genesis 12 ᐸ

Hello, I am Abraham. God changed my name from Abram and made it Abraham, which means, "Father of many nations." This was what God promised me and He fulfilled His promise to me.

When Noah's sons spread in different directions, each group looked for foreign gods, like the sun, moon, animals, or rivers to worship.

I love God. He is my friend. My wife, Sarah, loves God too. God said to me, "I want you to go on a very long journey." He made wonderful promises to me.

My wife and I obeyed God and were not afraid because of our faith in Him who always helps us. We did as God told us and left together with my nephew, Lot. We took with us our herds of camels, herds of cattle, and flocks of sheep. Finally, we arrived at Bethel, the land God had chosen for us. It had green valleys and flowing rivers. I lived there with my nephew, Lot, and we each had our herds of cattle and large flocks of sheep. There were not enough green pastures for all our animals and our herdsmen started arguing over the land.

I said to my nephew, "My brother, Lot, what I want the most is that we both live in love and peace. You can choose the best land you see and let us not have any quarrelling between you and me, or between your herdsmen and mine, for we are brothers. Is not the whole land before you? Please separate from me. If you take the left, then I will go to the right or if you go to the right, then I will go to the left."

Lot was selfish; so he chose a beautiful well-watered place filled with green pastures.

God promised Abraham that one day he will have children and many grandchildren and that they will own Canaan, the promised land.

The Birth and Marriage of Isaac
Genesis 21

Hello, this is Abraham again.

My wife, Sarah, was very sad because we did not have any children.

God promised us a son a long time ago but now we are very old.

One afternoon, when I was **99** years old, the Lord appeared to me and with Him were two angels. They looked like humans and I did not know them. The Lord said to me: "You will have a son."

Indeed, Sarah became pregnant and gave birth to a baby boy. I called him Isaac. We were both very happy. Isaac grew up and was always helping me with work.

One day, a strange thing happened. God told me, "Abraham, take your beloved son, Isaac, and offer him to Me as a burnt offering." I did not understand God's purpose for this, but because I loved God very much, I listened to Him. I took my son and we walked for three days to the place God had told me. I prepared the altar and put the wood on it; then, I tied my obedient young son and placed him on top of the wood on the altar.

I stretched out my hand and took the knife to slay my son, but the Angel of the Lord held my hand back and stopped me from doing so. He showed me a ram, caught by its horns in a tree, so that I would offer it instead. No one understood why God asked me to do this, until the Lord Jesus Christ, the only Son of God, came to the earth and His Father offered Him on the cross for our sins.

A Wife for Isaac: One day Abraham sent the oldest servant of his house, who was in charge of all that he had, to look for a wife for Isaac.

The servant stopped near a well and prayed to God saying, "May the girl that comes to the well and gives my camels water to drink be a wife for Isaac."

Indeed, a young girl came to the well. Her name was Rebekah, and she asked the servant. "Do you want water for your camels from the well?" The servant knew straight away that God wanted her to become Isaac's wife.

Jacob and Esau
Genesis 28

Hello, I am Jacob. My older brother, Esau, and I are twins. Our parents are Isaac and Rebekah. My brother was born with a lot of hair; so, he was named Esau, which means hairy. He grew up to be a skillful hunter.

My father wanted to bless Esau, since he was the firstborn, but my mother, Rebekah, wanted me to have that blessing. One day, while my brother went hunting, my mother put skins of animals on my arms and around my neck. As my father was very old and could not see well, he thought that I was Esau when he touched my arms, and thus, he blessed me with his special blessing.

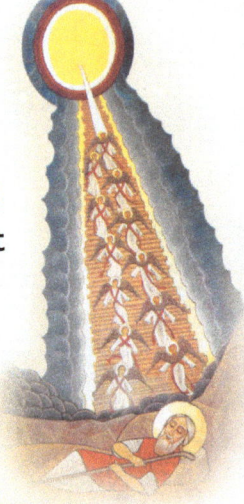

When my brother Esau discovered this, he was furious and hated me for taking his blessing. I had to flee to my uncle Laban's, home. He lived in a city far away. On my way there, I slept in the desert, as I was extremely tired and it was night. I put a stone under my head for a pillow and lay down to sleep. That night, I had an amazing dream. I saw a ladder. It's top reached to heaven and the angels of God were going up and down on it. The Lord said to me, "I am with you, I will take care of you and keep you wherever you go." In the morning when I woke up, I said, "Surely the Lord is in this place!"

At Uncle Laban's House
Genesis 29–33

Hello, this is I, Jacob, again. I arrived at my uncle, Laban's house. My uncle had two daughters, Leah and Rachel. I fell in love with Rachel and asked to marry her. My uncle told me, "If you shepherd my flocks for seven years I will let you marry Rachel."

Indeed after seven years of shepherding, I got married. The bride was wearing a veil that covered her face. In the morning, I discovered that she was Leah and not Rachel. I loved Rachel and my uncle let me marry her too, in return for another seven years' service.

After many years, I decided to return home. I was very worried! I wondered if Esau was still angry with me. When I saw Esau, I knelt before him and so did my family. He ran towards me and hugged me. We became good friends.

I Became a Slave in Egypt
Genesis 37

I am Joseph. My father, Jacob, had twelve sons. My father loved me more than all his other children and gave me a beautiful and colorful tunic. My brothers were jealous because my father did not give them beautiful tunics like mine.

One day, I told my brothers of a dream I had: "I dreamt we were in a field at harvest time, and your sheaves of grain bowed down to my sheaf." My brothers were outraged and they hated me. They said to me: "What do you mean? Do you actually think that we will bow to you?"

They thought among themselves of a way to be rid of me; so, they threw me in a dry well! When they saw Midianite traders passing by, they pulled me out of the well and sold me to them. The traders took me with them to a faraway country, Egypt. My brothers told our father, Jacob, that a ferocious animal devoured me.

In Egypt, the traders sold me to a rich man named Potiphar. He was the captain of the guard. I served him well. God was always with me, and therefore, I succeeded in everything I did.

One day, the rich man for whom I worked, put me in jail because his wife falsely accused me. I had not done anything wrong.

I Became the Second Man in Command in Egypt after Pharaoh
Genesis 39–50

In prison, I used to help the keeper of the prison and the prisoners by interpreting their dreams for them.

One night, the Pharaoh of Egypt had a dream. He saw seven fat cows coming out of the river, and then, seven thin cows came and ate them. Pharaoh also had another dream where he saw seven fat heads of grain and then seven thin ones spring up and atet the fat heads.

Pharaoh was disturbed by the dreams and could not sleep. "What do they mean?" he wondered!

Pharaoh heard that I was good at interpreting dreams, so he called me. God guided me to interpret Pharaoh's dreams. I told Pharaoh, "There will be seven years without rain, and there will not be enough food for the people. You have to store up food for these coming bad years." Pharaoh was pleased to have his dreams interpreted; so, he put me in charge of Egypt and its storag. We started storing food, so there would be plenty when the famine started.

I brought my father and brothers to Egypt so they would have enough food. I cried when I saw them and kissed them all as I missed them very much.

After my father's death, my brothers were afraid that I might want revenge because they were so unkind to me. I told them, "Do not be afraid. Am I in the place of God? You intended to harm me but God intended it for good. Do not be afraid. I will provide for you and your little ones."

I am Job

Job 1

I am Job. The whole world has heard my story. Have you heard it too? I will tell you my story so when you go through troubles, you may remember it and trust in the Lord.

I was a very rich man and I loved God very much. I was always trying to do everything that pleases Him. I grew up in the land of Uz in Arabia, east of Canaan at the time of Jacob, son of Isaac, son of Abraham. I was very happy and very thankful to God.

I had an amazing family and I used to pray for each member and present daily offerings to God on behalf of each one of them.

I had everything, but Satan, the enemy of God, asked God to allow frustrating things to happen to me. I went through painful trials. I lost all of my possessions and my seven sons and three daughters all at once. I also lost all that I possessed—sheep, camels, oxen, and donkeys. Even my health was affected and worms filled my body. I was saddened by what had happened, but I still loved God and was thankful to Him. I used to praise God during the painful times, saying, "The Lord gave, and the Lord has taken away; Blessed be the name of the Lord" (Job 1:21).

Three friends of mine came to comfort me, but instead, they made me even sadder. They insisted that what happened to me was because I had committed serious sins that were hidden from people but known to God. God asked me many questions to reveal to me His wisdom and power and to show me man's weakness.

God did not leave me to die in my pain, but He appeared to me and gave me more than I could have imagined. He gave me double what I had lost in possessions and also the same number of sons and daughters.

Question: Did Job stop loving God?

My Name is Miriam.
I Rescued My Little Brother
Exodus 2

Hello, I am Miriam. Do you have a younger brother? I had one. I used to care for him and play with him. Let me tell you how God saved his life through me.

Do you know my brother? He is very famous. I will give you a small hint: he was put in a basket that floated in the Nile River. I think you know him now. Yes! It is Moses!

Many years after Joseph's death, a new Pharaoh ruled over Egypt. He was very harsh and made us work as slaves. He ordered us to move very big stones and build him a great temple. He also made us make bricks all day in exchange for very little food. We were called, "the Israelites."

Pharaoh felt that we kept on growing in number and that we may be dangerous for him and Egypt in the future. So, Pharaoh commanded that every newborn son should be killed.

My brother was born and my mother wanted to keep him. He stayed in the house for three months, but as his voice began to be heard, mom feared that Pharaoh's soldiers might hear him and come into our house and kill us all. So, she put him in a basket and left him to float in the river. She asked me to watch after him from a distance. I was praying that the Lord would protect him, and when there was no one passing by, I would run and care for him.

I saw Pharaoh's daughter, the princess, swimming near the beach. She saw the baby in the basket and loved him very much. She decided to take this Israelite baby to live with her in the palace. She called him Moses, which means drawn out of the water.

I asked for God's help and then went to the princess and bravely offered my help by saying that I was happy to take care of the child for her. She agreed. I hurried to my mother and brought her to the princess who gave her Moses to nurse him and paid her money to care for him.

Moses Sees the Burning Bush
Exodus 2–3

Hi, my name is Moses.

I was brought up in the palace of the Pharaoh of Egypt as a son to His daughter. One day, I saw a cruel Egyptian man severely beating a Hebrew man. I attacked the Egyptian man and he died. I buried him in the sand. The next day, I was trying to reconcile two Hebrew men who were fighting. The guilty one said to me, "Do you want to kill me just like you killed the Egyptian?" I said to myself, "Oh dear, what I did yesterday is known. If Pharaoh finds out, he will kill me." To save my life, I ran away to a land called Midian, and there, I married a woman named, Zipporah, and worked as a shepherd tending flocks of sheep.

One day, I saw a small bush that was on fire but the fire did not burn it up. God spoke to me from the bush and told me to take of my shoes because the land on which I stood was holy.

He also told me, "Return to Egypt and tell Pharaoh to set My people free so they can worship Me in the desert." I thought I was unable to do what God asked of me, as I was not a good speaker. God promised me that He would help me and He told me to take my older brother, Aaron, with me.

I am Pharaoh, a God on Earth
Exodus 5–11

Do you know me? I am the greatest man on earth. I consider myself like a god. No one can stand against me. I was surprised when two Hebrew men (Moses and Aaron) asked to meet with me for an important and urgent matter. I agreed to meet them. They told me, "God is telling you to let the Israelites leave!" I threw them out and ordered that heavier work should be given to the people of Israel.

Moses and Aaron returned and asked me the same thing again. I refused their request and Aaron threw his rod on the floor in front of me and it turned into a snake. I sneered at him and called in the Egyptian magicians. They also threw their rods on the floor and turned them into snakes. However, Aaron's snake ate all the other snakes!

Many terrible plagues came upon us and I did not agree to let the Israelites go out of Egypt.

1. The water of the river turned into blood. We could not drink and all the fish died.
2. There were frogs everywhere!
3. We were bitten by lice.
4. There were flies everywhere!
5. The animals got sick and died!
6. Festering boils broke out on the Egyptians and what was left of their animals.
7. It rained hail and fire at the same time.
8. The locusts ate all the plants and the leaves.
9. There was darkness everywhere and no one could see where they were going.

Despite all these plagues, I continued to resist releasing the Israelites (God's people).

Question: What was the 10th plague?

The Passover Lamb
Exodus 12

When God allowed darkness to cover the land, no Egyptians could even move. Instead of Pharaoh letting us go to worship the Lord, he said to me angrily, "Get out of my sight and make sure you do not appear before me again for in the day you see my face, you shall die!" I answered him, "I will never see your face again!"

God asked us to eat a special meal that night. That meal was the Lord's Passover, and was to be celebrated every year to remember how God led us out of Egypt.

God told us that every Israelite household should take a lamb that is one year of age, slay it, and put some of its blood on the sides and on the top of the doorframes of their house. The Lord said that He will pass through Egypt and strike the firstborn of every household, but he would pass over the houses covered by the blood of the lamb. Those covered households would not be destroyed by the 10th plague. At midnight, there was a great cry in all the households of the Egyptians.

Finally, after this great plague, Pharaoh called me and Aaron by night and said, "Rise, go out from among my people, both you and the children of Israel. And go serve the Lord as you have said. Also, take your flocks and your herds, as you have said, and be gone, and bless me also."

The Passover Feast: The Lord Jesus Christ is the Lamb that was slain for your sake to set you free from Satan and allow you to pass over to the heavenly joy.

The People of God Crossing the Red Sea
Exodus 14

Hello again; it is me, Moses. What great and joyful news! Aaron and I will tell you all about it.

Pharaoh regretted letting us go; so, he sent an army after us. We continued to walk until the Lord told us to camp near the Red Sea. We were trapped! We heard the sound of Pharaoh's army behind us. The Red Sea was in front of us and the mountains surrounded us from the left and from the right. Everyone was frightened and cried out, saying, "Were we not better off serving the Egyptians than dying in the desert?"

I told them, "Do not be afraid. Stand still and see the salvation of the Lord. The Lord will fight for you, and you shall hold your peace." I lifted up my rod and stretched out my hand over the Red Sea and it was divided and dry land appeared in the midst of it. The people of God walked on the dry land and crossed the sea with a wall of water on their right and on their left.

After we all crossed the sea, the Lord asked me to stretch out my hands over the sea again. I did as I was told and the waters returned and covered all the Egyptian army and the horsemen that came into the sea after us. They all drowned in the sea. The Israelites saw the great power of the Lord and how He delivered them with His care. They all trusted in the Lord.

My sister, Miriam, sang beautiful praises while playing the timbrel. I am very happy that the Church dedicated the First Canticle in the Midnight Psalmody (praises) to remember the great work that the Lord has done for His people.

Bitter Water Becomes Sweet
Exodus 15

After we were brought out of the Red Sea, I led the people into the eastern wilderness and three days later, we arrived to Marah. The people were very thirsty, but when they drank from a spring, they realized that the water was very bitter. They complained to me, saying, "What shall we drink?" I cried out to the Lord and He showed me a tree. I cast the tree into the water and it turned sweet!

The Wood of the Cross:

This little tree is a symbol the cross of our Lord Jesus, which makes our hearts filled with the sweet water of grace and joy amidst the tribulations of the world.

The People of God in the Wilderness
Exodus 16–17

Hello again; it is me, Moses. What great and joyful news! Aaron and I will tell you all about it.

God overshadowed us in a pillar of cloud at daytime to protect us from the sun and led us through a pillar of fire at night.

We came to a place where there was no water and the people were thirsty. I asked God, "What should I do?" He answered: "Strike the rock with your rod." I did as I was told and water came out from the rock and they all drank.

Food for the Body and Soul:

The Lord cared and supplied food for our bodies. Will He then not care and supply the spiritual food for our souls? Our Lord Jesus Christ gives us His body and blood as spiritual food that offers eternal life.

A War with Amalek
Exodus 17

Hello, I am Aaron, Moses' older brother. I will tell you the story of how we conquered Amalek's army.

We attacked the army. The soldiers were giants and very strong. My brother told Joshua, "Choose for us some men and go out to fight Amalek." Moses, Hur, and I went up to the top of a hill. Moses had his rod in his hand; and so it was, when Moses held his hand up, we would conquer; and when he let his hand down, Amalek conquered. When Moses got tired, he sat on a rock. Hur and I supported his hands from each side, just like on a cross. We continued until sunset. That is how Joshua conquered Amalek.

We too, if we have faith in the cross, God will grant us victory over our enemies. The devil and his demons are giants just like Amalek and his army.

Question: How can you offer help to your brother, sister, and friends?

Moses on the High Mountain—Sinai
Exodus 20

Hello, I am Moses. When we were living in Egypt, we followed the Egyptian laws, but when God took us out of Egypt, He gave us new laws to follow. He asked me to go up to the top of a very high mountain—Mount Sinai. I spent forty days there with God and I was fasting. God told me what He wanted His people to do. He gave me Ten Commandments written on two tablets of stone (the tablets of the covenant). He wanted us to be His children and to get ready for living with Him.

The very first commandment was to love the Lord your God, because He loves you and you will live with Him in His embrace. The rest of the commandments taught us to set apart the day of the Lord, so you can praise Him joyfully just like the angels; To love your dad and mom and obey them, then your house will become a church. Do not act in a way that is unfitting for a son or daughter of God. For example: Do not kill, do not steal, do not lie, and do not desire that which is not yours.

Question: What are the tablets called that God gave Moses?

The Golden Calf
Exodus 31–32

My dear child, I am Moses. You will not believe what the people of God did when I was away from them. I was on top of the mountain for a long time and they thought that I had died. They asked my brother, Aaron, to make a golden statue of a calf, which the Egyptians used to worship, so they would worship it instead of God, as if it was the calf that delivered and led them all this way!

Finally, I came down from the mountain carrying in my hands the two tablets of stone with the commandments God had given me. I was furious when I saw the people of God singing and dancing in front of the golden calf that I threw the two tablets on the floor. I prayed to God that He may forgive them and He forgave them.

The Tabernacle of Meeting
Exodus 35–36

This is Moses, again. God, lovingly, asked me to make a special place for worship. It's name was the "Tabernacle of Meeting." God described everything He wanted to put in it: a golden altar, golden lampstand, and a table for special holy bread of which no one was allowed to eat except the priests. God, Himself, came and blessed the tabernacle with His presence to make it holy. A cloud covered the Tabernacle of Meeting and the glory of the Lord filled the tabernacle.

It is God's house. People come to it to thank God and to pray to Him. People worship God in the Tabernacle of Meeting; it was like the church for them.

The tabernacle was divided into two parts and separated by a beautiful veil:

1. The most holy: this symbolized heaven and in it was the "Ark of Covenant."

2. The holy place: it had the golden lampstand in it because Christ is the light of the world, the golden altar, which symbolizes the offering of prayers, and the holy bread because Christ is the heavenly bread.

Outside of the tabernacle, there was a bronze altar where sacrifices were offered and a laver where the priests washed themselves when offering sacrifices.

Question: Does the Tabernacle of Meeting look like your church?

The Ark of the Covenant
Exodus 25

I am Moses. God assigned me to make the Ark of the Covenant and to put in it the tablets of the Covenant, a plate with Manna, and my brother Aaron's rod. This Ark of the Covenant was a symbol of God's presence in the Tabernacle of Meeting. Also, whenever we moved to a new place, we always took the Ark with us.

The Ark of the Covenant was a beautiful box made from a special kind of material called acacia wood and is covered with gold from the inside and out. It has rings on each side for the poles to go into, so that the priest could use them to carry the Ark. It is called the Ark of the Covenant because it contains the tablets of the Covenant. No one was allowed to touch the Ark except for the priests. On its cover, which is called the mercy seat, there were two statues in the form of cherubim, which are beautiful looking angels. God would speak to me from between the cherubim.

A Cloud Leading the People
Exodus 40

Hello, I am Moses. God assigned me to take His people on a very long journey. Do you know how I used to find the way? I would look up and see a special cloud that God would move especially for us to lead us on our way. Whenever the cloud lifted itself from the Tabernacle of Meeting, we would follow it and move to the place God would choose for us.

In the New Testament, God gave His Church His Holy Spirit to lead the way. The Holy Spirit descended on the disciples on the day of Pentecost. The Holy Spirit gives us power, guides us, and reminds us of Christ's work for the salvation of the world.

Question: How do you know God's will so you can walk on the right path?

The First High Priest
Exodus 4:14–17

Who was the first high priest? I am Aaron, the older brother of Moses the prophet and Mary, the prophetess.

My brother, Moses, refused to come to Egypt to ask Pharaoh to let God's people go to the wilderness to sacrifice to the Lord, because he could not speak well.

God wanted me to be with him, and speak for him, for God was with my brother's mouth and mine.

God gave me the authority to perform miracles. I took Moses' rod, cast it down before Pharaoh, and it became a serpent.

I was with my brother until the day I died. I was one hundred and 23 years old.

I sinned when the people asked me to make an idol in the shape of a golden calf to worship it, because Moses stayed too long up on Mount Sinai.

Nevertheless, God forgave me, and appointed me the first high priest for the children of Israel, and all the priests after me are my offspring.

I was in charge of the house of the Lord—the tabernacle of meeting—offering sacrifices and burnt offerings to God, and praying on behalf of the people.

I confess that sometimes I was jealous of my brother Moses, because he was the leader.

When I died, my son, Eleazar, was appointed high priest.

Prayer: Grant me, O Lord, to work in your Church with my brethren and my fathers, as has Aaron with his brother, and to pray for the people.

Spies in the Promised Land
Numbers 13–14

My name is Caleb. I will tell you about the adventures I had with my friends in the promised land.

The congregation camped at Mount Sinai for about a year. When the cloud lifted, Moses, our great leader, told us about the promised land, the place we were supposed to go.

The leader sent for me. In no time, I found myself with eleven friends, for he had chosen a representative from each tribe. Moses, the prophet, told us: "Brethren, the Lord instructed me to send twelve explorers to survey and inspect the land that He had promised us. Therefore, I wish that you go there, learn all about it, and tell the people.

- "Are people dwelling in these countries strong or weak?
- "Are they few or many?
- "Are the cities open like camps or surrounded by fences and strongholds?
- "What type of land is it: fertile, with lots of trees, or rather like a desert?

"Moreover, if possible, please bring back a sample of the fruit of the land."

We found the land very good, and all its trees full of fruits. However, we faced a difficult problem: Joshua and I were very happy, but the other ten were sad. They said that the congregation will not be able to enter this land because the people who dwell there were strong, like giants, and we would be like small grasshoppers in their sight.

We returned to share our findings with the congregation, and Joshua and I carried one cluster of grapes on a pole. We also brought pomegranates and figs. We told the congregation, "We trust that the Lord is with us and is watching over us."

When we returned, we told the people of Israel all about the land and how exceedingly good it was. We showed them the fruits that we brought with us. I told them let us go take this land for our possession for we were able to do so. But the other men said, "There are giants in this land, and we will never be able to overcome them."

The entire congregation lifted up their voices screaming, weeping, and complaining that night, saying, "If only we had died in the land of Egypt!" They began to complain about Moses and Aaron saying, "Why has the Lord brought us to this land? Does He want us to die, so our wives and children should become their slaves?" Therefore, they said to one another, "Let us select a leader and return to Egypt."

Joshua and I tried to comfort the congregation, but they threatened to stone us with rocks.

Sadly, this generation died and did not enter the promised land, except for Joshua and I.

Question: What do you do when you are scared?

I Did Not Obey God
Numbers 20:1–13

Hello again! I am Moses. I love God very much, and have always obeyed Him. God made me lead His people out of Egypt, and saved us from the bondage of Pharaoh.

He guided us in the wilderness and gave us all that we needed, despite the people's endless complaining. Let me tell you about one of these instances when the congregation complained about God Himself, my brother Aaron, and me.

The people started complaining when there was no water in the wilderness, saying, "We wish we had died like our brethren who died! Why have you brought us into this wilderness? To die?"

The Lord heard them and told me, "Take the rod, and gather the congregation together. Speak to the rock before their eyes, and it will yield its water."

So, I gathered the assembly together before the rock, and said to them, "Hear now, must we bring water for you out of this rock?" Then, I lifted my hand and struck the rock twice with my rod, and water came out abundantly.

The Lord was not happy with me because I was not precise in heeding His word. He had asked me to speak to the rock, but in my anger caused by the wrath of the children of Israel, I struck the rock twice instead of speaking to it. Therefore, God punished me, saying, "You shall not enter into the promised land."

Question: What do you do when you are angry?

The Bronze Serpent
Numbers 21

I am Moses. I will tell you about a sad event that happened in the wilderness.

People complained persistently about God and me, and were becoming increasingly violent. So, God allowed poisonous serpents (snakes) to bite them. Many died, and God's people were scared.

I rushed to God, crying, because I loved the congregation.

God said to me, "Make a serpent of bronze, and set it on a pole in a high place. The people who were bitten by the serpents may look at it, and I shall heal them and make them well again."

In obedience to God, I made the bronze serpent, and all those who looked at it, whether men or women, old, young, or children, were healed right away.

This bronze serpent represents the cross of our Lord Jesus Christ who saved us from death.

Question: If you were sick, whom do you ask to heal you?

Balaam and His Donkey
Numbers 22

I am Balaam. Do you know me?

I am a Midianite of the people who worship idols. I was a magician. I heard about God and the wonders that He did for His people since they left Egypt and were led by Moses, and then crossed the wilderness until they moved close to Moab on the way to the promised land.

I had a donkey to ride as means of transportation, but did not know that he could speak!

God's people terrified the king of Moab. He sent for me so that I could help him, saying, "I know that you are able to harm God's people. Come and curse this people, and I will give you a big reward."

I got on the road riding my donkey. Suddenly, the donkey stopped and would not move. I struck him hard, trying to make her go. He spoke to me saying, "What have I done to you, that you have struck me?"

Finally, God opened my eyes, and I saw the Angel of the Lord, with His drawn sword in His hand. I listened to Him speaking God's words.

I was very sad I had struck my donkey violently, but was glad he had stopped me. For the Angel of the Lord warned me that I should not speak against God's people!

I prophesied about the birth of Christ (Numbers 23:7-10), His resurrection (Numbers 23:16-24), the Pentecost (50th Day) (Numbers 24:1-14), and about preaching of the Gospel (Numbers 24:15-19).

Regrettably, I betrayed the children of Israel later, and was killed while fighting against them.

The Kiss of Death
Deuteronomy 33–34

It is Moses, again, here! I want to tell one last story which happened to me before I died. After about forty years in the wilderness, we finally made it to the border of the promised land.

Although I was aware I would not enter the promised land with the congregation, I was still delighted because they would enter it and enjoy it. I want to remind you of the things which God had done with your fathers, and His commandments and laws.

As I turned 120 years old, God asked me to go up to the top of Mount Nebo, so that I may see the land of which He swore to Abraham, Isaac, and Jacob to give to their descendants.

I went up by myself, to see the promised land from afar and to praise God.

Did you know?
1. The Lord came, took Moses' spirit, and buried him.
2. No one has arranged for a funeral for Moses. Neither was anyone from his family or the congregation with him when he died. However, the Lord Himself took care of his soul and body.
3. The devil wanted to disclose the location of Moses' body for the Jews to worship him instead of worshipping God, but Archangel Michael rebuked him in the name of the Lord.
4. No one knows where Moses' body is located.
5. The Jews call Moses' death, "the kiss of death," because they say that God came down, kissed him, and took his soul.

Joshua the Son of Nun
Joshua 1

I am Joshua, the son of Nun. I am so happy I had the opportunity to live with my master, teacher, and beloved, Moses.

Never have I thought that I could live without my beloved teacher, Moses, much less take his place to lead the people to the promised land.

The Lord spoke to me saying, "Moses My servant is dead. Now therefore, arise, go over this Jordan, you and all this people, to the land which I am giving to them.

"No man shall be able to stand before you all the days of your life.

"As I was with Moses, so I will be with you.

"I will not leave you nor forsake you.

"Be strong and of good courage…

"This Book of the Law shall not depart from your mouth.

The Lord your God is with you wherever you go."

I divided the land among the tribes and departed this world happy when I was 110 years old, because I had successfully done my job.

Question: How did Joshua help the people?

Two Spies on the Roof
Joshua 2

I am Joshua. Do you remember that Moses had chosen me as one among the twelve explorers to survey the promised land?

Caleb, my colleague and friend, and I came back joyful, and trusting that we will enter the beautiful land, which God had promised Abraham to give to his descendants. We will now cross the river Jordan.

I asked two men to enter the great city of Jericho and gather information about it. Let me introduce you to one of the two spies so he can tell you what happened with them:

We were scared at first, not knowing where to go, or to whom we should speak. We were afraid the king would hear about us and kill us. We searched for a place and found a house built on the city wall. A woman named Rahab lived there. We asked her to accommodate us, and offered to pay her whatever she wants. Much to our surprise, she recognized that we were of the children of Israel, and knew all about us since we came out of Egypt. Then, we heard knocking on the door. She asked us to go up on the roof and hide between the stalks of flax.

The door opened, and soldiers came in, asking for us. Rahab told them that we had just left, and went toward the gate to return to the East Bank. So, the soldiers hurried to leave to pursue us.

Rahab told us about Jericho's king and its people, and how they were terrified of us. She knew we would eventually conquer the city and asked us to spare her and her family of any harm. We promised her that no family members who enter her house would be harmed, on one condition: she must bind a cord of a scarlet color (i.e., color of blood) in the window.

This scarlet cord is a symbol of the Lord Jesus Christ, who protects us.

The Walls of Jericho Collapse
Joshua 2

I am Joshua. I wish to enter the promised land and give it to the tribes.

The priests went toward the river carrying the Ark of the Covenant and were followed by the people. As soon as their feet rested on the waters of the river, the water flow coming from upstream was cut off, uncovering a path on dry land, thus allowing the congregation to cross the Jordan.

The Canaanite kings were speechless when they heard about Moses and the children of Israel crossing the Red Sea forty years earlier. They also heard how the same people defeated mighty giants, and had extensive military experience, even though they had no combat experience.

When we crossed the Jordan River under my command, and got close to them, they were very afraid—I dare say terrified! They wondered, saying, "Who are these that the waters of the Jordan river stop for them, and the bottom of the river dries up instantly so that they may cross in the middle of the river?"

Now, we wanted to enter the city of Jericho. Orders were given to close the gates shut, and no one was allowed to enter or exit. Many climbed on the walls of this great city to see how this people woud enter.

God showed me (Joshua) the method by which they can enter Jerico. We had to march around the great city of Jericho once daily for six days. Seven priests would march before the Ark of the Covenant carrying rams' horns and preceding the people. On the seventh day, we marched around the city seven times, and the priests blew the trumpets, and the people shouted with a great noise. That is what we did, and immediately, the walls fell and the people entered Jericho.

Rahab and her family were saved because she hid the two spies that I (Joshua) sent to survey the land. Her house was distinguished by a scarlet (i.e., red-colored) cord that was tied to the window. Rahab's house became a symbol of the church, which is protected by the blood of Christ, so that its members—the believers do not perish.

Question: How could Joshua enter Jericho?

The Sun Stands Still in the midst of Heaven
Joshua 10

I am the sun. I appear first thing in the morning and go down and disappear at the end of the day.

One of these days, Joshua went to fight enemies in Gibeon—five armies in total. God told him that he should not fear them.

Indeed, God cast down large hailstones from heaven on the five armies, and they scattered. Thus, Joshua's army overtook them, but needed more time to win the war. Joshua prayed, and God ordered me—I the sun—to not go down, and wait longer in the midst of heaven until God's people prevail in battle.

Joshua was so happy when he divided the promised land amongst the tribes. He did not take his share of the land until every tribe got its own share.

Know that the believer does not find happiness until his brethren are happy. Our Lord Jesus Christ died on the cross and was happy to do so to grant us heavenly life through the cross.

Question: Do you think that God has power over everything?

A Woman Leads a Great Battle
Judges 4

I am Deborah. I usually sit quietly under a palm tree and feel God's presence with me. Many came to me for judgment in their disagreements. I was also a prophetess, eager to relay God's message to my people and reveal His will to them.

I have never received any military training using weapons as did commander Barak. When foreign people attacked our people and stole their crops, God told me that it was time to go to war with them.

I told Barak, "Go and deploy troops at Mount Tabor, and get ready for war." And Barak said to me, "If you will go with me, then I will go; but if you will not go with me, I will not go!"

Barak was afraid to go to war, for most of his soldiers were infantry, with no chariots; but the enemy had nine hundred chariots of iron, were able to move fast, and could be driven over the soldiers, thus killing them.

I was not afraid, not because I was trained in battles, but because I trusted in God's words to me that we must engage in battle.

When the enemy saw me, they mocked me and made fun of the army that had no chariots, and thought that they could easily win in no time! But, God intervened, and they were troubled, left their chariots, and fled. Our army engaged them in the battle and won.

We all praised God and thanked Him for caring for us.

Question: What is the reason for Deborah's victory?

Is The Angel Saying Something Funny?
Judges 6

I am Gideon. Do you know me? I was a simple farmer, who would hide in a cave. I threshed wheat in the winepress to separate it from hay in order to hide it from the Midianites so that they would not take it from me. All of a sudden, I saw the Angel of the Lord appearing to me, saying, "The Lord is with you, you mighty man of valor!"

I was astonished by what he said, and thought he was joking! I am not at all a mighty man of valor, but just a simple peasant, weak, afraid, and hiding in a cave!

I also did not feel that God is with me because the Midianites were destroying our crops, and were taking our sheep and cows, leaving us with nothing to eat.

I was so confused when the Angel of the Lord told me to lead an army and drive out these thieves! How can that be when I had never fought a war? I am just a simple peasant, who comes from the weakest family, and I am the least in my father's house!

I asked him to show me a sign, to make sure that God would help me.

I shall put a fleece of wool on the threshing floor; and asked that the dew fill the fleece only, while all the ground stays dry. And it was so. When I rose early the next morning and squeezed the fleece together, I wrung the dew out of the fleece, and filled a bowlful of water.

I then asked for the opposite to happen. And indeed, the next morning, it was dry on the fleece only, but there was dew on all the ground. I knew then that God was with me.

Question: What was the joke that the Angel of the Lord told Gideon?

85

The Strangest Weapon Which Was Used in Battle
Judges 7

I am Gideon. I was a judge, commander of the army, and ruler in Israel, before there was any reigning king in it. I will tell you about the strangest weapon that was used in battle.

Thousands of Midianites gathered against us, and sought to fight us. God chose me and told me, "You need a very small army to fight the Midianites."

The Lord's command surprised me, but I still heeded Him. I had thirty-two thousand men with me. I proclaimed in the hearing of the people, saying, "Whoever is fearful and afraid, let him turn and not come with me to war." And 22,000 of the people returned, and ten thousand remained with me.

But the Lord said to me, "The people are still too many." So I brought the people down to the river. And the Lord said to me, "Everyone who drinks from the water with his hands, you shall take them to your army; but everyone who gets down on his knees to drink, do not take with you."

And the number of those who used their hands to drink water was three hundred men. I was afraid because the army became too small, but the Lord reassured me that He would help me.

I felt very courageous when I went out with those three hundred men with me. I gave my soldiers torches and pitchers and said to them, "These are your weapons; take care of them." They were very astonished, but did not say anything. On the same night, the men broke all the pitchers at the same time, which made a great noise, lit all the torches at once, and so it was very bright, and cried out, "The sword of the Lord and of Gideon!"

The army of the enemy was afraid and fled. My small army fought thousands of enemy soldiers, and God helped them, and the victory of the war was theirs!

Samson
Judges 13–16

I am Samson. My name means, "the small sun."

The Israelites worshipped many pagan gods, so the Lord allowed that they become slaves to the Philistines for forty years. Then, He had compassion upon them, and so He gave me power and appointed me as a judge to save them.

My mother was barren (could not bear children). The Angel of the Lord appeared to her and asked her to listen to God's word, that she is going to become pregnant and give birth to a son, who will be a Nazirite (which means dedicated to serve the Lord) from his mother's womb, and will deliver Israel from the hands of the Philistines. Nazirites could neither drink alcohol, nor cut the hair on their head.

The Lord blessed me, and I became a very, very, strong man.

God helped me tear the strong ropes with which I was tied. I also tore the lion's jaws (his mouth) with my bare hands when I was on the way to ask a Philistine girl to marry me. A few days later, when I was going back to my father's house, I found a beehive full of honey in the mouth of that same lion. took the honey, ate some on the way, and gave some to my parents without telling them anything about the lion.

What happened to me became a proverb, "Out of the eater came something to eat, and out of the strong came something sweet." I triumphed over many of the enemy soldiers by myself. One day, I fell in love with Delilah, even though she was on the side of our enemies. She insisted, and found out that if I cut the hair on my head, I would lose God's support, and will become weak, because I would be disobeying Him.

While I was asleep, the enemy came and shaved my hair. They took me captive, humiliated me, and mocked me during their festivities. They laughed at me and bound me up like an animal to a mill in prison.

After some time, they did not notice that my hair grew long again. They brought me to a big temple to make fun of me, where they were gathered to celebrate one of the idols. I prayed to God and said, "O Lord God, remember me, I pray! Strengthen me." I took hold of two big pillars of the temple, and brought them together, and so the building fell on about three thousand of God's enemies. I lost my life with them.

I would like to whisper something in your ear, "When your life is beautiful with Christ in prayers, keep it to yourself, that it may grow and multiply more and more in His knowledge."

Question:
Who made Samson strong?

Naomi and Ruth
Ruth 1

My name is Naomi. I lived during the days of the Judges. There was a famine in the land because it had stopped raining for a long time. Elimelech, my husband, and I were forced to travel to Moab, along with our two children. Both our children married Moabite girls. One of them was named Ruth. I had hoped to have a grandchild.

My husband died, and a few years later, so did both my sons. I was very saddened and felt troubled by my loneliness. I decided to go back by myself to my home country, Bethlehem, to live among my family.

Ruth loved me so much, because she loved God. She told me, "Do not insist, for I will not leave you, for wherever you go, I will go; and wherever you lodge, I will lodge; your people shall be my people, and your God, my God. Where you die, I will die, and there will I be buried. Nothing but death will part us."

Ruth did not leave me, but came with me on a long journey, leaving her home country to be with me and to help me. So, God blessed her.

I was very sad because my husband and both of my sons had died.

One day, Ruth went to the fields to search for food for both of us to eat, and there she met a man named Boaz, who fell in love with her and married her.

God was very pleased with Ruth because she was kind and loved her mother-in-law, and so our Lord Jesus Christ was from her offspring.

Question: Name an act of love that you have done for one of your relatives?

I Hear a Voice at Night
1 Samuel 2–12

I am Samuel. My mother, Hannah, was very sad because God did not give her a child for many years. She prayed to God, and He promised her that He would answer her prayers and grant her desire of having a child. My mother gave birth to me, and when I was a little boy, she brought me to the Tabernacle. I grew and became a youth, and was serving and helping Eli the priest.

One night, when I was in bed, I heard a voice calling me, saying, "Samuel, Samuel." I ran to Eli and said, "Here I am father." And he said, "I did not call; lie down again." And I went and lay down. Then, I heard the same voice, yet again, a second time… and a third time, "Samuel, Samuel!" Then Eli perceived that the Lord had called me. Therefore, Eli said to me, "Go, lie down; and it shall be, if He calls you, that you must say, 'Speak, Lord, for Your servant hears.'" So I went and lay down. When I heard the voice, I worshipped God and said, "Speak, for Your servant hears. Say what You want me to do, and I will do it."

The Lord told me what He intends to do in Israel. When I grew up, He made me His prophet. The Lord was with me as I was growing up. All the people and the leaders loved me. I loved God and was happy praying and offering sacrifices.

God blessed me and blessed the people. The Philistines, who were worshippers of idols, could not overcome Israel all my days. Even the cities that they captured from Israel were returned. I was a judge and God gave me wisdom.

My motto was, "As for me, far be it from me that I should sin against the Lord in ceasing to pray for you; but I will teach you the good and the right way."

A Shy Peasant Becomes King
1 Samuel 8–9

I am Saul, son of Kish. Allow me to tell you my story candidly. As Samuel grew old, all of us, old and young, loved him and respected him, for he was the man of God. Samuel's two sons were judges in Beersheba, but unfortunately, they did not follow his ways.

I was not too concerned about this matter, for I was a simple farmer, ignorant about political matters. I heard that the people asked Samuel for a king to lead them. This demand saddened Samuel's heart, not because someone would take his place, but because the people wanted to foster a reputation of greatness and dignity, boastful about their king as did other neighboring nations.

I found out that God asked Samuel to listen to all that the people were saying to him, even though I was not paying much attention to such matters.

I was strong, very tall, and handsome. I was shocked and amazed when the prophet told me that God had chosen me to be king over His people, for I was shy, and never dreamt to become a leader, not even a ruler of a small village. I hid myself because I was not fit for this position.

Samuel, the prophet, introduced me to the people and said, "This is your king; heed him." In the beginning, I conducted myself in obedience to God and His righteous prophet. But after a while, pride took over my heart and thoughts, and I did many things that were not pleasing to God. I made many mistakes, some of which was my fondness of greatness, and the desire to practice the priestly tasks. Therefore, I offered a sacrifice with the excuse that Samuel did not come on time to offer it.

Samuel was sad for me because I had gone astray and done evil. God rejected me and sent Samuel to make the youth, David, a king. I tried to kill David many times, even though he had saved my life and the life of the people.

Question: Why did God reject Saul?

David, the Little Boy
1 Samuel 16–17

I am David, the little boy. I was playing Psalm 23 on my harp, "The Lord is my shepherd; I shall not want."

My father's sheep gathered around me, and were looking at me. I felt there was dancing in my heart. All of a sudden, one of my brothers came and told me, "Our father is asking for you, and is waiting for you." I answered, "To whom shall I leave my friends, the sheep?" He replied, "Our father said to leave them with one of the shepherds, and to come right away, for there is an enjoyable surprise at home. Samuel, the prophet, is visiting!"

I immediately left my sheep and went home with my brother. As soon as we entered, I found my father and all my seven brothers. Samuel. the prophet, welcomed me and kissed me. Then, he took the horn of oil and poured the oil on my head, and I felt the power of the Spirit fill me.

The prophet congratulated me and said, "The Lord has chosen you to be king over His people."

When the prophet left, I asked my father, "Why did he not choose one of my older brothers? I am young and inexperienced." He answered, "I have introduced them to him, but every time, the Lord would say, 'Do not look at his appearance, for man looks at the outside, but the Lord looks at the heart.'"

It was so strange that the Spirit of the Lord departed from Saul the king, and often times, a distressing spirit would overcome him and trouble him day and night. He would relax for a while when he listened to pleasant music.

Saul would ask me to play music for him because of my love for it, especially when I composed tunes for the psalms and praises to the Lord.

I wrote beautiful songs called psalms to praise God and to proclaim His love for me, and my love for Him.

Did you know? David was the father of a great king named Solomon the wise?

In the Battlefield
1 Samuel 17

I am David. One day, my father, Jesse, asked me to go check on my three older brothers, for they were accompanying Saul, the king, in the battle. There, the mighty Goliath could be heard challenging God's people and even mocking God, saying that he would kill anyone who would dare fight him. Goliath was huge and strong, standing about nine feet tall. Everyone was greatly afraid of him—even the king!

I went to the battlefield and saw Goliath humiliating the Lord of hosts. I was exceedingly zealous, and asked, "What shall be done for the man who kills this Philistine and takes away the reproach from Israel?" My brothers heard what I said and know of my courage and zealousness, because I use to keep the sheep safe from wild beasts, like lions and bears. One day, while tending to my father's sheep, a lion came desiring to eat a lamb from among my sheep. I snatched the lamb from the lion's mouth right away and killed the lion. My brothers feared for my life, but I went ahead to meet the king.

Saul did not recognize me, for he was in a sad state when I was playing music for him. He would not even bother to look at me, or ask me about my family. Even though I was young, I was not afraid of Goliath because I trusted that God always helps me.

I went to fight the giant, who was wearing full military attire and was armed with a sword. As for me, I only had a sling and five smooth stones.

Let me tell you what happened to me when I went to the battleground!

A Young Man with a Sling, or a Giant Warrior?
1 Samuel 17

I am David, the youth and shepherd. I am getting ready now to go to battle against this poor giant, who is mocking my Almighty God.

Saul asked me to wear his military gear, but the bronze helmet was too heavy on my head. I could not breathe when I put on the shield and the sword was too heavy, so much that I was unable to walk. I asked the king to be excused from wearing this military attire.

I bent down to grab my staff, which I had left on the ground, chose five smooth stones from the brook, and grabbed my sling. The king looked at me, bewildered, thinking what is this poor young man doing?

I moved toward the mighty giant, whose military attire was heavier than I! Goliath stopped mocking the Lord my God and began to move slowly toward me, for he thought I was a play puppet.

He began to laugh, disdaining me and saying, "Is there no one smaller than this boy in Israel's army to come and meet me?"

Amid his loud laughs and the mocking of all the Philistines' army of me, I prayed and struck his forehead with a smooth stone from my sling, and he fell on the ground.

I ran and took Goliath's sword, not sure if his mouth was laughing or screaming. I stood over his body, which was on the ground, and cut off his head!

Question: How do we destroy Satan—the evil one who fights God?

A Strange Friendship!
1 Samuel 18

I am Jonathan, the son of Saul, the king. I was a warrior, not fearing death, and people loved me. David was my friend and I loved him very much. Truly, David won the respect of the people and the royal court, even more so than my father, the king. He really deserved it, for he saved my father and my country from the gigantic Goliath.

I gave David my clothes, sword, and bow as my gift to him and as a sign of our friendship, to use in times of peace and war. David and I were friends who cared and loved one another. It was said that my soul was knit to the soul of David, and I loved him as my own soul.

My father, Saul, cautioned me that David would take the kingdom away from me. But, I considered my love and friendship for him to be much greater than the throne of this kingdom, and more valuable than obeying my father, for he (my father) planned to kill him (David) many times, but the Lord protected David from my father!

My father was not pleased to see the women sing and dance in celebration of David's victory, saying, "Saul has slain his thousands, and David his ten thousands," which basically meant that David was more courageous than Saul, and was killing more people in battle than Saul—which was true!

In his anger, my father tried to strike David with a spear more than once, but David escaped from him. One time, my father sent messengers to David's house to watch him and to kill him in the morning. I told my sister, Michal, who was also David's wife, of our father's plan, and so Michal asked David to flee right away before morning, and she let him out down through a window.

My father and his soldiers kept chasing David to kill him. One night, while Saul was asleep in a cave, David came and took his spear and water pitcher, which was next to him, without harming Saul, because Saul was the Lord's chosen king.

Did you know? When Jonathan and Saul's other children died in battle, Saul was very sad, threw himself on his sword, and died. As for David, he cried a lot because of the death of Jonathan, his friend, and Saul, Jonathan's father, despite what Saul had done to him.

David the King
2 Samuel 6

Do you know me? I am David. I did not try to become king after Saul's death. Instead, I asked permission of the Lord to go to Judah. Once there, the people celebrated me as their king.

I faced many hardships internally, from within the country, and from abroad. Internally, Saul drove the statesmen to hate me; and abroad, I had to fight many battles to bring back the strength of the kingdom amongst other nations. God was with me in all of this.

I made Jerusalem the kingdom's capital. However, my most important task was to help the people return to worshipping God, for they had drifted away from God during Saul's reign, and after Samuel, the prophet's, death.

I wanted to bring the Ark of God close to me. I had the priests carry it and enter the city of Jerusalem with it. I walked before them, dancing and praising God, full of gladness and joy. I loved God, and God loved me exceedingly.

God loves you too. You should be very happy knowing that.

It was said of me that my heart was like God's heart, observing God's word, and was patient with His enemies. I was a poet and a musician. I used to sing two psalms at the start of every day, and before I went to sleep, even when I was fleeing from Saul.

Despite this, I was lazy and fell into some great sins that I had not committed before when I was young; however, in the end, I repented and returned to my God.

Question: What made King David rejoice?

David Falls Into Sin, and Repents
2 Samuel 11–12

I am Bathsheba. God bestowed me with amazing beauty. Uriah, my husband, was a commander in King David's army. He was loyal and true to his people as to the king.

One day, David walked on the roof of his palace, saw me, and sent me one of his men to summon me to go and see him.

Even though I was married, David desired to take me as his wife. He succeeded! He had his men send my husband to fight on the frontlines so that he may die in battle.

When David did this, he did not heed the Lord's command, which disappointed God, and so He punished him. God allowed our son to die.

God never stopped loving David, for He wishes that everyone be saved. He sent Nathan, the prophet, to David, so that he may confess and repent.

The merciful God granted David and I another son named Solomon, who was the wisest king in all history, and who built the Lord's temple.

Question: Is there a person without sin?

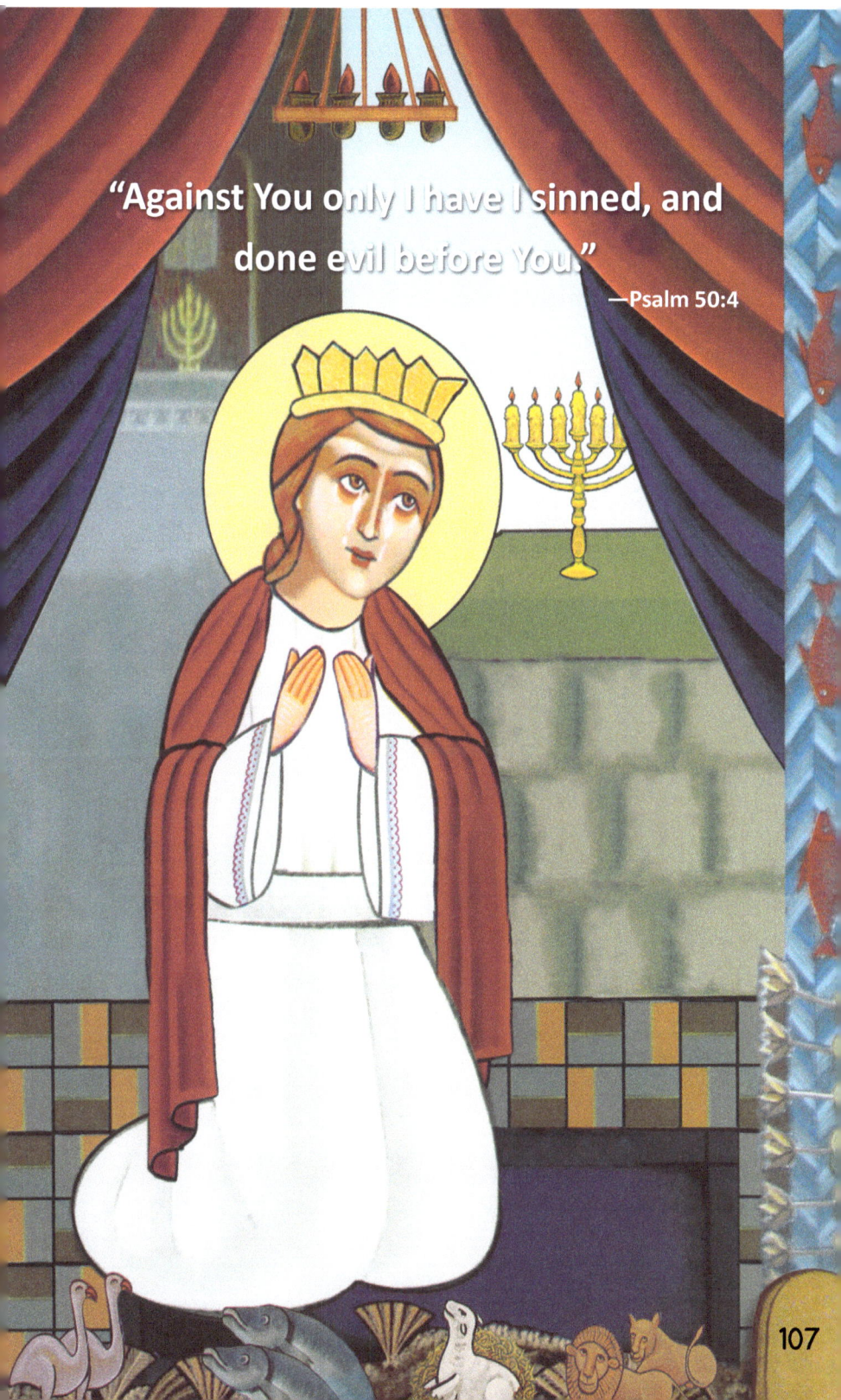

The Kindness of King David
2 Samuel 15–16

I am David. Absalom, my son, wanted to be king instead of me. He rebelled against me, and publicly declared war on me. I withdrew from Jerusalem to the Mount of Olives, walking barefoot, weeping, and covering my head. All the people who were with me covered their heads and wept as well.

On the way to the Mount of Olives, a man from Saul's family approached me. His name was Shimei. He and his servants were cursing me, and throwing stones at me, saying, "Come out! Come out! You bloodthirsty man, you rogue!"

One of my men told me, "Why should this dead dog curse my lord the king? Please, let me go over and take off his head!" I answered him, "Let him alone, and let him curse; for so the Lord has ordered him. It may be that the Lord will look on my affliction, and that the Lord will repay me with good for his cursing this day."

And I continued my journey with my men.

Question: What did the Lord Christ say about the meek? (See Matthew 5:5)

A Son Rebels Against His Father
2 Samuel 18

I am Absalom. My father, David, the prophet and king, is a man who loved God and the people. Since I was a little boy, I used to sit by him while he sang his psalms day and night. He played them on his lovely harp. I used to look at him when he would stand for prayers, and I would see his face as the face of an angel of light.

I was very handsome, and very proud of my tall stature and thick hair. Do you know that I used to get a haircut at the end of every year and my hair weighed five pounds?

My father (David) made mistakes. He had more than one wife. Unfortunately, he treated my oldest brother Amnon better than me. His mother is not my mother. Amnon sinned, which saddened my father's (David's) heart, and mine. My father, David, made a mistake for not punishing Amnon. This was not fair; so, I killed Amnon, fled to another town, and went to live with my grandfather. My father, David, was angry with me and would not speak to me at all. Too much time had passed and my father had not forgiven me, so I got extremely angry with him and decided to kill him.

I began to interact with the people in humbleness to attract them to me, and so many of them loved me. I rebelled against my father and declared war on him. My father withdrew from the royal palace, and also from Jerusalem.

In my foolishness, I thought I would be happy to kill my father and sit on the throne in his place. I went to battle against my father's very small army. My father had commanded his soldiers not to touch me. My father really loved me!

I was sure I was going to kill my father and defeat his army. I did not realize that God was with him, and the devil controlled me. I was shocked when my army was defeated.

I tried to escape by riding on a mule, but a thick tree branch got stuck in my hair—the hair of which I was so proud, and the mule went on, leaving me hanging in the air.

None of my soldiers came to my rescue, for they were running away, completely baffled.

I felt that what I intended to do to my father would befall me. Indeed, a man saw me, and told Joab, the commander, who thrust three spears through my heart. I closed my eyes! Oh! What a bitter moment! You would not imagine how sad my father was when I died this way. I was only 27 years old!

Prayer: Grant me, O God, that I may resemble You, for you were obedient to Your mother and Saint Joseph. (See Luke 2:5)

King Solomon the Wise
1 Kings 1–3

I am Solomon. Before my father, David, died, he commanded his men to enthrone me as the king, and that I must ride on his horse for the people to know that I am their new king.

Zadok, the priest, anointed me with holy oil and the priests blew the horns so that the people may know that God had chosen me. The people rejoiced and prayed that God may let the king live a long life.

God appeared to me in a dream asking, "What would you like most? Health, food, or victory over your enemies?" I replied, "My dear God, I ask You to make me wise, so that I may serve Your people in honesty."

God was pleased with me and gave me great wisdom as I had asked. He also gave me things for which I did not ask, such as riches, glory, and honor.

One day, two women and a child came. Each one of the women claimed that the child was her son. I asked the swordsman to divide the child in two, and to give one half to each one of them. One of the women screamed and asked that the child not be divided, but be given to the other woman. Then, I knew that the woman who loves the child and wanted to preserve his life was his real mother; so, I handed her the child.

Question: What does it mean that someone is wise? Who is able to grant you wisdom?

The Blessings of Building the Temple
1 Kings 8

I am King Solomon. I wanted to make my father David's dream come true, which was to build a house for the Lord. He left me a lot of building materials, such as gold and silver to build the house of the Lord. My father strengthened the kingdom. Therefore, I had no need to go to war against any nation—near or far.

In the four hundred and eightieth year after the children of Israel had come out of the land of Egypt, in the fourth year of my reign over Israel, I selected thirty thousand workers and sent them to Lebanon to bring wood and building materials, eighty thousand to quarry stone in the mountains, and three thousand to supervise the people who labored in the work. This way, I was able to build the temple in seven years, before the watchful eyes of the world, who considered it one of the world's wonders!

Most of the temple was covered in gold. The altar, the lampstands, and the door hinges were made of pure gold. The Ark of the Covenant was covered in gold inside and out, and the table of showbread was also covered in gold.

I met with the elders of Israel and all the heads of the tribes. The priests brought up the Ark of the Covenant, the Tabernacle of Meeting, and all the holy furnishings. There were so many sacrifices.

Everyone celebrated the dedication of the temple for seven days.

I prayed saying, "May your eyes be open toward this temple night and day, toward the place of which You said, 'My name shall be there.'"

Prayer: I thank you, O Lord, for You keep the doors of Your house always open, and You allow us to partake of Your holy body and blood, as the divine sacrifice for our salvation.

The Queen of Sheba Visits Solomon
1 Kings 10

I am the Queen of Sheba. Many kings feared me and my kingdom was very rich.

I heard about King Solomon and how he was wiser and richer than me. He wrote three thousand proverbs and more than one thousand songs. I neither envied him, nor was I jealous of him, for I knew that God had given him wisdom, understanding, grace, glory, and riches.

I rejoiced when I learned that many great people heard about him, and so, I also desired to see him and hear him.

I came to him with a very great entourage, and camels that bore gold, precious stones, and gifts. I also came with hard questions to ask him to answer.

My journey to Jerusalem on camels lasted more than one month. I marveled at what I heard and saw. I confessed to him that I did not believe the words until I came and saw with my own eyes, and indeed, the half was not told me. His wisdom and prosperity exceeded the fame of which I heard.

King Solomon greatly attended to me and answered all my questions. We established trade agreements and friendships between our countries.

I praised God with all my heart before I left him, saying, "Happy are your men and happy are these your servants, who stand continually before you and hear your wisdom. Blessed be the Lord your God, who delighted in you, setting you on the throne of Israel! Because the Lord has loved Israel forever, therefore He made you king, to do justice and righteousness." Then I went back to my country and talked to everyone about him.

Question: What is the source of Solomon's wisdom and glory?

The Wisest Man Carries Out the Most Foolish Behavior
1 Kings 11

I am Solomon. The Holy Bible witnessed about me that I was the wisest king in history.

I loved God and was heeding His word. I asked Him for wisdom, and He gave it to me, and with it, He gave me riches, honor, and glory. God never deprived me of my free will.

Regrettably, of my own will, I married many pagan women. I thought that by so doing, I would develop family ties with all the kings around me, and thus, live in perfect peace and harmony. However, these wives made me worship idols. I broke the most important command that God gave us. I began to build altars for idols, worship them, offer them sacrifices, and pray to them.

Who could have imagined that I was the son of David, the one whose heart was after God's heart? David, my father, rejoiced in whatever God wanted!

During my reign as king, Israel was at the high point of its greatness, richness, and glory. In foolishness, I have introduced the worship of idols to Israel. This saddened God, the true God; He was angry with me because of what I had done. He said that after me, the kingdom will be divided, and someone who is not my descendant will reign over the greater part of this divided kingdom.

I reigned for forty years, and when I died, the kingdom was divided during the reign of my son, Rehoboam; and later, both kingdoms collapsed.

Who could fix what I have destroyed other than our Lord Jesus Christ, Son of David, who alone is without sin?

Rehoboam and Jeroboam
1 Kings 11–12

I am Rehoboam, son of Solomon. I went to Shechem after the death of my father. There, all Israel assembled together to crown me so that I may become king.

They asked me, saying, "Your father was harsh with us, do not be as harsh as him, but be gentle, and we will be your loyal servants." I rejected the advice of the elders, and answered them, "If my father was harsh with you, I will be even harsher." Regrettably, this was the advice of my wicked friends. I did not listen to the advice of the people who are older and wiser than me and my friends.

So Jeroboam, who was at odds with my father, became their king. And as such, the kingdom was divided into two: The Northern Kingdom was comprised of all the tribes with the exception of the tribes of Judah and Benjamin. The Southern Kingdom consisted only of the tribes of Judah and Benjamin.

Jeroboam was anxious that the people will long for the temple in Jerusalem, go and worship there, and leave his kingdom. He built two altars, one in Bethel and one in Dan, and crafted a calf of gold for each altar.

All the kings of Israel (Northern Kingdom) were evil. After a long period of time, they made a treaty with Syria, a nation that worshipped idols. Later, both these nations fell under the rule of Assyria. It was said that Assyria used every means of savagery and humiliation to oppress the people when it occupied a country.

Concerning Israel, Assyria sent many people of Samaria to distant nations, and sent some foreigners to Samaria, so that the Jews would forget their language and faith. So, in effect, the people of Samaria, the capital of Israel, were a hodgepodge of Jews and all kinds of pagan Gentiles. They only believed in the Five Books of Moses (the Torah), not accepting the remainder of the books. They also mixed the worship of the living God with the adoration of pagan gods. All this caused a bitter enmity between them and the Jews.

As for the kingdom of Judah, it boasted that its king was a descendant of David, that it kept Jerusalem, the city of God as its capital, and that the Temple of Solomon was in its midst. Some if its kings were righteous, and some were evil.

The kingdom of Judah should have learned a lesson from what happened with the kingdom of Israel, as it fell under the Assyrian captivity. Instead, the kingdom of Judah fell into many evils, relying on the belief that God will not allow the destruction of His city and temple and will not humiliate its kings because they were David's descendants.

The prophets warned the kingdom of Judah numerous times, just as they had warned the kingdom of Israel, but they did not listen, and even persecuted those prophets.

When Nebuchadnezzar became the emperor of Babylon, he captured the kingdom of Judah, and took the honorable, nobles, and skilled laborers captives, and sent them to Babylon.

Judith Saves Her People
Judith

I am Holofernes, the general of the Assyrian army. Esarhaddon, king of Assyria, sent me to besiege the Jewish stronghold, Bethulia, and cut off the water supply to the city. The leaders and people in Jerusalem were miserable. Everyone feared me, and all the Middle Eastern nations were frightened of me.

The captain of my army was named Achior. As I sought to fight God's people, Achior told me, "The Lord will defend God's people, and we will not be able to defeat them so long as the Lord is with them." I became extremely angry and ordered that Achior be delivered into the hands of the Jews.

Achior told them of all that he had said to me, giving them assurances of victory if they behaved as befits God's people, and that victory or defeat was not contingent upon my military equipment or plan to annihilate them by thirst, but was based upon their relation with God. I will now let Judith tell you what happened after that.

I am Judith, the widow. It was said that I was wise, beautiful, and God loving. I broke into the camp of Holofernes with my maid, without letting the leaders know my intentions. I spent time in meditation with God, and was fasting. I asked the leaders to pray for me. Indeed God was with me and I killed Holofernes. Then, I returned to Bethulia with his head in my food bag.

The city was transformed into a heavenly icon with everyone praising and thanking God, for He swapped their decision of surrendering as slaves to Assyria, and for Achior to join them.

The Assyrians fled in weakness, and the people celebrated continuously for three months.

Ahab, King of Israel, and the Evil Jezebel
1 Kings 16:29–34

I am Ahab, king of Israel. I fell in love with the beautiful Jezebel, the daughter of the king of the Sidonians and priest of Baal, and I married her. Jezebel's only concern was to push me to work with her to discourage the people from worshipping God, and to spread the worship of Baal in all Israel. Thus, she allowed many priests of Baal to live in Israel.

Jezebel, the Baal priests, and I encouraged the statesmen to worship Baal. It was difficult for us to contest the worship of the living God, who had saved Israel from the bondage of Pharaoh, took care of them in the wilderness, and granted them victory over the Gentiles and dispersed them.

We began to tell the people, "We did not forget that God is the God of war, who defeated Pharaoh and his armies, who defeated the nations which lived in this land. But Baal is the rain master: he orders the sky and it rains, and therefore prevents famines. He is also the one that gives us sons and daughters, and makes the trees fruitful. Whoever does not worship Baal will trigger a famine, cause the women to be barren, and the trees to not bear fruits. Whoever does not worship Baal will be killed immediately! We worship him, love him, and offer little children as sacrifice to him, so that he may be pleased with us."

Because the people were very afraid of Jezebel and me, they began to worship Baal and forgot God.

Question: What is the first of the Ten Commandments? (See Deuteronomy 6).

Elijah, the Prophet, and Ahab, the Wicked King
1 Kings 17

I am Elijah. God chose me as one of the Old Testament prophets. He sent me to meet Ahab, king of Israel. Ahab rejected God's word more times than all the kings before him combined.

I said to him, "Tell the Lord that you are sorry, or else there will be no rain, and the crops will not grow, and your people will be famished."

Regrettably, Ahab laughed, and did not listen to the word of the Lord. He thought to himself, "I have no need for God, I need Baal, for he is the rain master, and provider of fruit. Let Elijah say whatever he wants. After all, no one has dominion over the rain except Baal."

Ahab, the king, was astonished that there was no rain for three and a half years, and he became angry with me and wanted to arrest me.

God said to me, "Get away from here and turn eastward, and hide by the Brook Cherith, which flows into the Jordan." God commanded the ravens to feed me every day. The ravens brought me bread and meat in the morning and in the evening, and I drank from the brook.

It happened after a while that the brook dried up because there had been no rain in the land. Thus, I found no water in the brook to drink.

Elijah, the Prophet, and the Poor Widow
1 Kings 17:1–16

Elijah, here, again! The Lord said to me, "Arise, go to Zarephath, and dwell there. See, I have commanded a poor widow there to provide for you." I arose and went to Zarephath. I saw a widow there gathering sticks. I called to her and said, "Please bring me a little water in a cup, that I may drink." As she was going to get it, I called to her and said, "Please bring me a morsel of bread."

The woman had a small quantity of flour and a little oil. She said to me, "I am gathering a couple of sticks that I may go in and prepare a small cake for myself and my son, that we may eat it, and die."

I said to her, "Do not fear, God will provide food for us. Go make me a small cake first; and afterward make some for yourself and your son." She went away and did according to my word; and we all ate for many days. Since that day, the bin of flour did not empty, nor did the jar of oil decrease until it rained.

The woman thanked God for He cared for her and her son on account of my request of her.

Question: Do you believe that God provides you with food, water, and all that you need?

Reviving the Widow's Son
1 Kings 17:17–24

I am a poor widow. I was taking care of Elijah, one of the great prophets. All of a sudden, my son became sick and died because of the seriousness of his illness.

Elijah's heart was moved. In all faithfulness, he asked God to revive my son. He took my son out of my arms and carried him to the upper room where he was staying in my house; for I had prepared it for him especially to lodge when he blessed us. Elijah laid him on his bed. Then, he cried out to the Lord, and stretched himself out on the child three times, and said, "O Lord my God, I pray, let this child's soul come back to him."

The Lord heard Elijah's voice and my child's soul returned, and he was revived.

Elijah took the child and brought him down from the upper room, and said, "See, your son lives!"

I said to Elijah, "Now by this I know that you are a man of God, and that the word of the Lord is in your mouth is the truth."

Prayer: I thank you, O Lord, for You love me. You gave me Your body and blood to overcome death.

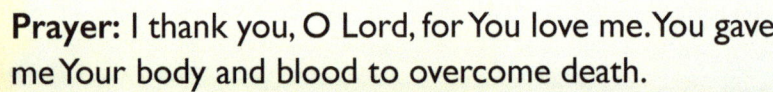

Elijah, the Prophet, Destroys the Worship of Baal
1 Kings 18

I am Elijah. There was a severe famine in Israel because of the drought and lack of rain for three and a half years. The Lord asked me to present myself to Ahab, the king, so that I may send rain on the earth.

I went to Samaria. Then, it happened, when Ahab saw me, he said, "Is that you, O troubler of Israel?"

I answered courageously and calmly, "I have not troubled Israel, but you and your father's house have, in that you have forsaken the commandments of the Lord and have followed the Baals. Now therefore, send and gather all Israel to me on Mount Carmel, the prophets of Baal, and the idol worshippers."

Ahab sent for all the children of Israel and gathered the prophets together on Mount Carmel. When everyone was gathered, King Ahab stood along with the prophets and priests of Baal to pray to Baal, asking him to send rain. But, it never rained! I said to the king, "Let us both go and each one of us builds an altar of stones, and we will pray together to see if Baal or God answers." I poured water on the sacrifice that I was going to offer.

Ahab and all the Baal priests prayed and danced to Baal. They even cut themselves for Baal to hear them, but nothing happened!

I prayed to God, and fire came down from heaven as a sign of God's satisfaction, and consumed the wood and the stones, and the excessive amounts of water was absorbed, even though everyone knows that water puts out fire.

Immediately, thereafter, it started to rain. The crops began to grow! The people thanked God, returned to Him, destroyed the altars of Baal, and rejected the worship of idols.

Question: Do you believe that God answers your prayers?

The Vineyard of Naboth, the Jezreelite
1 Kings 21

I am Naboth and I love God with all my heart. I lived in an area called Jezreel. I inherited a vineyard (a field of grapes) from my father and ancestors. This vineyard was located next to the gardens of King Ahab's palace.

The king desired to take my vineyard and annex it to the garden of his palace. He asked me to sell him the vineyard. I declined, for I was afraid that the king would build an altar to Baal in the vineyard, since he had stopped worshipping God and was offering sacrifices to Baal. Also, I had to hold onto the inherited land of my fathers, as would any other Jewish man, so that every tribe would conserve its share in the promised land.

The king returned to his palace depressed, and would not eat any food. Jezebel, his evil wife, asked him why he was sad. He told her about what had happened. She comforted him saying, "Arise, eat food; I will give you the vineyard of Naboth the Jezreelite."

Jezebel sent letters to the elders and the nobles asking them to accuse me of saying bad things about God and insulting the king, so that they would kill me. The elders did as Jezebel had sent to them. They proclaimed a fast, judged me, stoned me with stones, and the king took possession of my vineyard.

It happened that God sent Elijah to Ahab, saying, "Have you murdered and also taken possession of the vineyard? … In the place where dogs licked the blood of Naboth, dogs shall lick your blood…. And the dogs shall eat Jezebel in the same vineyard."

The king tore his clothes, wore sackcloth, fasted, and went about bewildered, refusing to speak to anyone. God had compassion on Ahab and told Elijah, "See how Ahab has humbled himself before Me? I will not bring the calamity in his days. In the days of his son I will bring the calamity on his house."

Practice: Remember that it shall be done to you as you do to your brethren.

A Chariot of Fire Transports Elijah the Prophet
2 Kings 2

I am Elijah, the Prophet. I have grown very old, and it is time for me to go and be with God in heaven. Let Elisha, my disciple, continue the service to help the people walk in the obedience of God.

Elisha and I were in Gilgal when I said to him, "Stay here, please, for the Lord has sent me on to Bethel."

But, Elisha said, "I will not leave you, and will go with you to Bethel!"

When we went down to Bethel, the sons of the prophets came out to Elisha and said to him, "Do you know that the Lord will take away your master from you today?"

Elisha replied, "Yes, I know; keep silent!"

I said to him, "Elisha, stay here, please, for the Lord has sent me on to Jericho." He insisted and said, "I will not leave you!" So, we came to Jericho.

The same thing happened in Jericho with the sons of the prophets, for they asked him the same question. Thus, he answered, "Yes, I know; keep silent!"

I tried one more time that he remains there, but he said that he would not leave me. So, we went onto the river Jordan. While we stood by the river, I took my mantle, rolled it up, and struck the water; and it was divided this way and that way, and we crossed the river.

I asked Elisha, "Ask! What may I do for you, before I am taken away from you?" Elisha said, "Please let a double portion of your spirit be upon me."

I said, "You have asked a hard thing. Nevertheless, if you see me when I am taken from you, it shall be so for you." Then, it happened, as we talked, that suddenly a chariot of fire appeared with horses of fire, and separated the two of us. I went up by a whirlwind into heaven, and Elisha saw it, and cried out, "My father, my father, the chariot of Israel and its horsemen!" I threw my mantle to Elisha, and he became a great prophet after me. God helped him with his service.

Question: Do you know who are those in heaven?

Elisha, the Prophet, and the Poor Widow
2 Kings 4

I am a poor widow. My husband died and I have two sons. I am in debt, but have no money to repay what I owe. The creditor threatened me that he is coming to take my two sons to be his slaves.

Sad and weeping, I cried out to Elisha, the prophet, and told him, "My husband is of the sons of the prophets, but died while owing a debt. You know that he feared the Lord and loved Him. The creditor came to take my sons to be his slaves."

Elisha asked me, "What shall I do for you? Tell me, what do you have in the house?" I answered, "I have nothing in the house but a jar of oil, not enough for one meal."

Elisha said, "Go, borrow vessels from everywhere, from all your neighbors—empty vessels; And when you have come in, you shall shut the door behind you and your sons; then pour the little oil that you have into all those vessels."

I did as Elisha told me to do, and I kept pouring and pouring, and my sons were handing me the empty vessels, and the jar was not emptied until all the vessels were full. I said to my sons, "Bring me another vessel." But they said to me, "There is not another vessel." Thus, the oil ceased. Then, Elisha told me to go and sell all this oil to pay my debt, and buy what my sons and I need.

I thanked God who sent me the prophet to provide me with my needs.

Question: God guided Elisha to help the widow. Who is the one who helps your family?

Elisha, the Prophet, and the Shunamite Woman
2 Kings 4

I am Elisha. I would travel from town to town to visit the schools of the prophets in different places.

There was a town called "Shunem" on my way. A great woman who loved God lived in this town. She and her husband always welcomed me in their house every time I went to their town.

I had Gehazi, my servant, ask the woman if she was in need of anything from the king or the commander of the army. She answered that she dwells among her own people, and would not ask for anything for herself, for she has whatever her people have, and is happy when all the people are happy.

Gehazi said to me that the woman and her husband have no children, and have not asked that God provide them with a child. I rejoiced in them, for they do not ask for anything for themselves. I prayed for them, and God gave them a son.

Now it happened one day that their son became sick and died. The woman ran to me asking for my help. I prayed to God and He raised him from the dead and returned him to life another time. God can do anything!

Question: Is there anything that God cannot do?

Elisha, the Prophet, and Naaman, the Syrian
2 Kings 5

I am Naaman the Syrian, commander of the great army of Syria in Damascus. I was stricken with a horrible skin disease called leprosy.

Our maid, a young girl of the people of God, told my wife, "My lord should go to Samaria to see Elisha, the prophet of God, for he is capable to heal him of his leprosy, with the help of God."

I got into my chariot, took many gifts with me, and had a letter from the king of Syria to the king of Israel.

When the king of Israel read the letter, he tore his clothes and thought that the king of Syria was asking for the impossible, which is to get me healed of the leprosy. When Elisha the man of God heard that the king of Israel had torn his clothes, he sent to the king, saying, "Why have you torn your clothes? Please let him come to me, and he shall know that there is a prophet in Israel."

How marvelous! The young girl believed that Elisha could pray for me and I would be healed; yet, the king and all the religious men surrounding him did not believe that the God of Elisha could make the impossible happen.

Therefore, I went to meet Elisha, who told me, "Go and wash in the Jordan seven times."

I thought this was a joke, for in my country, there were two rivers whose waters are much better than the waters of the Jordan. But, one of my servants told me, "My father, please do as Elisha the prophet says."

I went down and dipped seven times in the Jordan, according to the saying of the Elisha, and the Lord healed me. My flesh was restored like the flesh of a little child. I knew then that there is no God other than the living God, who is in heaven.

I offered gifts to Elisha, but he refused to take any of them; so, I departed. While I was on my way, I heard someone running after me. It was Gehazi, Elisha's servant. I got down from my chariot, and said, "Is all well?"

He answered, "All is well. My master has sent me, saying, 'Indeed, just now two young men of the sons of the prophets have come to me. Please give them a talent of silver and two changes of garments.'"

I replied, "Please, accept, and take." I gave him two talents of silver in two bags, with two changes of garments, and handed them to two of my servants, and they carried them on ahead of Gehazi. But, Gehazi did not tell Elisha that he took silver from me, and lied to him.

So, Elisha said to him, "The leprosy of Naaman shall cling to you and your descendants forever." And Gehazi went out leprous from Elisha's presence.

Question: Are the two rivers of Syria better than the Jordan river, in which the Lord was baptized?

Elisha, the Prophet, and the Ax Head
2 Kings 6

I am Elisha. God made me the leader of the sons of the prophets. I loved them for they were my disciples. I visited them often in their schools and in their dwelling places.

The sons of the prophets were poor and simple, building their own houses themselves, so that it does not cost them anything other than their labor.

They asked me if they could go to the Jordan to cut down trees to build houses for themselves. When I agreed, they asked me to go with them. I happily consented.

However, the iron ax head of one of them fell into the water and sank. So, he cried out and said, "Alas, master! For it was borrowed, and I have no money to buy another."

So, I cut off a stick, and threw it in the river; and the iron head floated.

This is what our Lord Jesus Christ did when He saw that our souls sank in the waters of sin. He came down to us through the wood of the cross, so that we may be elevated above sin.

Practice: Remember that Emmanuel came down for you and was crucified on a wooden cross, so that you may be raised. Do not be fearful of sin or the devil.

Jonah and the City of Nineveh
Jonah 1

I am Jonah. I was dwelling in Israel. I love God with all my heart, and I obey Him. Amittai, my father, was a prophet. God chose me, too, to be a prophet.

Nineveh was the capital of the kingdom of Assyria (today's Iraq), one of the greatest cities in the East. However, the people there were evil. God wanted to give them a chance to repent and return to Him because He loved them.

One day, God said to me, "Go to Nineveh, and tell them that their city will be destroyed because of their wickedness."

I was very dismayed, for Nineveh was very violent with my people. I know that God is very merciful and will forgive the people of Nineveh as soon they repent.

For the first time in my life, I did not obey God's word. I decided to run away from Him to avoid going to Nineveh.

Instead of going to Nineveh to the East, I went to the seashore, and got into a ship to flee to Tarshish, which is in the West.

God sent out a mighty storm, and I knew that it was because of me. I wanted to save the sailors and the passengers, and so I asked them to throw me overboard and leave me to die because I did not obey God, so that they would not be killed by the tempest.

I told the truth to those on the ship, which is why God sent a big fish to swallow me, and keep me in his belly for three days, after which, I would get out and love even my enemies.

Jonah and the Big Whale [or Big Fish]
Jonah 2–4

God sent a great big whale that swallowed me. I felt as if I were in heaven. I prayed to my God and praised Him. I was full of joy and happiness. Three days later, the Lord ordered the big whale to vomit me onto dry land; and I learned to obey God!

I went to Nineveh, the city to which God had ordered me to go.

The king of Nineveh and its entire people repented and fasted for three days. God pardoned them and forgave them their trespasses.

Question:
Do you care that all peoples repent and return to God?

Blessed is Egypt My People
Isaiah 6–19

I am Isaiah, the Prophet. I was born in the royal family in the nation of Judah, more than seven hundred years before the coming of the Lord Jesus Christ. I loved God with all my heart, His people, His temple, and Jerusalem, His city. I was sad because of the evildoings of the king and his family, as well as the priests, those who labor in the temple, and even the people.

I was speaking to God just how a person speaks to his friend!

One day, a strong light shone upon me, and I was very happy. I knelt down before God, who started to talk with me and tell me about His plan concerning His people, and also the Gentiles. He said, "Alas, sinful nation. They have forsaken the Lord, they have provoked to anger, the Holy One of Israel!"

I cried, and with my eyes full with tears, I said, "What is the solution? Who can change the hearts? Who can uproot evil from the holiest city in the world?"

Despite the gloomy atmosphere in which I was, I felt I was the happiest man on earth at the same time. For in my sadness, God filled my heart with great joy when I saw the magnificence of His glory on the altar.

God spoke to me and said, "Do not be afraid, Isaiah. I love all of mankind. I will reveal to you what I intend to do, not only with Judah, but also with all peoples. I will come down and become man in the end of days, and will be crucified for the sake of the world, giving Myself as a sacrifice, and carrying the sins of the world."

My conversation with God filled my heart with joy. I believed that God, the lover of mankind, would implement this divine plan, for He is the God of the impossible.

Amid all these difficult conditions, God revealed to me events bound to occur:

First: The coming of Christ Jesus, the Word of God and Savior of the world.

Second: The Gentiles accepting faith through the Messiah, the Savior.

Third: The flight of the Holy Family to Egypt, and the building of an altar of God in it, as He said to me, "Blessed is Egypt My people."

Jehoash (Joash), the Child King
2 Kings 11

I am Joash. I was an infant when my evil grandmother, Athaliah, ordered all the children that were descendants of David to be killed, so that no one could take the throne away from her. She was exceedingly violent and arrogant. She gave the order, and did not care to ask for a list of names of those killed, for she could not imagine that anyone would dare disobey her.

My uncle, Jehoiada, the high priest, and my aunt, his wife and sister of King Ahaziah, hid me from my evil grandmother in a room in the house of the Lord. I loved the house of the Lord since I was a child, for in it, I was saved from the murderous Queen Athaliah, until I was seven years old.

Then, the great priest brought me and I stood on the pulpit at the altar. A great multitude of nobles and people came, and shouted, proclaiming that I was the king!

When the queen heard all the cheering at the altar, she came to investigate the matter. She saw me at the pulpit, with the crown on my head, and the guards surrounding me. She cried out, "Treason! Treason!"

Alas, the queen could not find anyone to stand by her.

The soldiers arrested my grandmother, the queen, cast her out of the house of the Lord, and killed her there. Thus, the people were relieved.

I love God, and heed His word.

King Joash, and the Repairing of the Temple of God
2 Kings 12

Once more, I am Joash. When I ascended to the throne, Jehoiada, the high priest, was handling the matters of the kingdom until I grew up and could manage the kingdom by myself.

I wanted to rebuild that which was destroyed in the temple of the Lord and make it beautiful and worthy of God.

At first, I asked that the priests handle this chore, but they were not up to the task, perhaps because the people lost their trust in them for they did not care to repair the damages of the temple all these years during the reign of the evil kings and Queen Athaliah?

I had to ask my scribe and the chief priest to work together to repair the damage to the temple quickly.

The people realized how much I cared, and so they made considerable amounts of contributions for this undertaking.

The people brought all the money and silver that they could to the house of the Lord, and used all the money to buy timber and hewn stone, and to pay the workmen. They completed the rebuilding of the portions of the temple of the Lord, which were destroyed, and made it beautiful.

Question:

Do you give to the Lord of your money?

The Evil King Ahaz
2 Chronicles 28

I am Isaiah, the prophet. God sent me to Ahaz, the evil king, who was enthroned king when he was twenty years of age. Ahaz loved the idols so much that he presented his own son to the gods as a sacrifice. He also ordered that the gates of the temple be shut, so that no one could enter and pray to God.

One day, Rezin, king of Syria and Pekah, king of Israel, conspired together against him. They besieged him in Jerusalem with their armies.

God sent me to him, so that he would not resort to foreign powers for help, but instead, put the matter into God's hands. But, he did not heed the voice of the Lord. Ahaz took gold from the house of the Lord, from the house of the king, and from the chiefs, and gave it to Tiglath-Pileser, the king of Assyria, to help him, but received no help.

The king of Assyria moved away, and so, the kings of Syria and Israel left the siege.

The king of Assyria attacked Samaria (the capital of Israel) and went on to Damascus, and killed Rezin, the king of Syria.

Ahaz heard of this and went to Damascus to offer obedience and submission to the king of Assyria. There, he marveled at an altar of idols and asked that a similar one be built and be placed in the temple of the Lord—effectively destroying the house of the Lord.

He shut up the doors of the vestibule of the temple, put out the lamps (the lights), and forbade burning incense or burnt offerings to the Lord.

In the last years of his reign, the Philistines conquered parts of his kingdom and the Edomites attacked him. When he asked for help from the king of Assyria, he did not get it, but instead, the king of Assyria distressed him. Now in the time of his distress, King Ahaz did not return to the Lord, but rather, became increasingly unfaithful to Him.

Question:

To whom do you resort when you run into a problem?

King Hezekiah
2 Kings 18

I am Hezekiah, king of Israel. I heeded God's word and was a servant to the Lord. I began my reign by restoring the temple and by cleansing it from all idol worship. I removed the golden statutes and destroyed the idols that the evil kings worshipped.

I celebrated the Passover in the exact prescribed manner of the Law. Not only did I send celebration invitations to the tribes of Judah and Benjamin, but also to the other ten tribes of Israel.

My era was known for the attack of Assyria on the entire region, and the falling of many nations under the rule of the Assyrians. Sennacherib, king of Assyria, sent a letter to the people of Judah, in which he insulted God and mocked His people and me. Then, one of the leaders of the Assyrian army, called Rabshakeh, besieged Jerusalem, so that King Sennacherib could enter the city effortlessly.

I covered myself with sackcloth, went into the house of the Lord, prostrated on the ground, and spread the letter before God. I also sent some of the leaders to Isaiah, the prophet, so that he may raise prayers for me.

God sent an angel to kill 185,000 Assyrian soldiers in one hour. Sennacherib, king of Assyria, returned home, ashamed and disgraced. As he was worshiping in the temple of his idol, his two sons killed him. Esarhaddon, his son, reigned in his place, and attacked the Medes and many other nations.

I fell sick. Isaiah came to let me know that I was dying. After he left, I prayed to God in tears. God asked Isaiah to come back and inform me that He had extended my life by fifteen years.

Question: How did Hezekiah defeat Sennacherib, king of Assyria?

163

King Josiah Finds the Book of the Law
2 Kings 22

I am Josiah. I was eight years old when I became king over Judah.

My grandfather, Manasseh, was evil. He reigned for fifty-five years. My father, Amon, reigned two years, and was killed by his servants.

I was so sad because so many people forsook God and worshipped idols. I loved God and was always willing to heed to His word. The great priest, Hilkiah, was my guide at my young age.

In the eighteenth year of my reign, I ordered that the temple be repaired and redecorated. However, I was unaware of the Book of the Law, for it had been lost for a long time. During the repairing of the temple, Shaphan, the scribe, found the Book of the Law.

They read it before me. I was sorrowful and regretted my sins and those of the people. I prayed to God that He would forgive me, and He did.

I gathered the priests, the leaders, and the people and personally read the Law of God. The people and I made a covenant to follow God and to keep His commandments.

Question: How can we know the right behavior whereby we ought to conduct ourselves?

Baruch, the Scribe
Jeremiah 36

I am Baruch. I was born in Jerusalem. I liked Jeremiah, the prophet, because he was the man of God.

In approximately the year 550 before the birth of Christ the Lord, the prophet called for me, and read out the word of God to me, which he had prophesied concerning the evildoings of the king and the people.

When I read what I had written to the people and to the leaders of the Jews in the house of the Lord, they were troubled.

And it happened that Jehoiakim, the king, heard of this, and one of the king's men read three or four columns of what I wrote. The king became very angry, cut the scroll, and cast it into the fire.

The prophet, Jeremiah, called me again, and instructed me to write what had been previously written, and added grave prophecies. I remained with him.

I was imprisoned with him when the enemy besieged Jerusalem, and we were both freed when the Babylonians occupied it.

I accompanied Jeremiah when the people seized him against his will, and I went to Egypt with him. We were both depressed because of what befell the city.

Prayer: O God, grant me the courage of Jeremiah and of his scribe, Baruch, so that I may fear neither people nor death, but be dismayed about the wicked who resist You.

The Prophet Jeremiah
Jeremiah

I am Jeremiah, of a village called, Anathoth. My father's name was Hilkiah. He was a priest. The people of my village despised me, and believed that I betrayed our nation because I flattered no one—not the priests, statesmen, or even the king!

God called me to the prophetic work since I was a child, saying, "Do not say, 'I am a youth.'"

I was telling everyone—king, leaders, and the people—"Repent and return to the Lord, or else, God will send armies of foreign nations to defeat you."

The people did not listen to me. Some men took me and cast me in a deep well so that I would not utter God's word.

Then, the king ordered his men to get me out of the well, but even then, I did not stop telling them what God expects of them.

The great king of Babylon came with his army, seized the people, and took them to a very far nation.

Despite my courage and candor, I was troubled because of my people. I wrote lamentations when I foresaw the destruction of Jerusalem and the captivity to Babylon.

I was called the lamenting prophet because I said, "O my soul, my soul! I am pained in my very heart! My heart makes a noise in me; I cannot hold my peace." I also said, "Oh, that my head were waters, and my eyes a fountain of tears, that I might weep day and night, for the slain of the daughter of my people!"

Question: How did God care for Jeremiah?

A Prophet Performs an Acting Part!
⥽ Ezekiel ⥼

Do you know me? I am the prophet, Ezekiel. The Lord chose me to perform an act!

Why are you astonished? God sent many prophets who spoke in every possible way to warn kings, dignitaries, priests, and peoples of the evil that they were committing. It is because of these evils that God allowed the burning of Jerusalem and the temple of the Lord, and that people were taken to far nations to be punished. Despite all of this, the people did not heed to the prophets' warning. Therefore, God sent me to act out a show, so they understand and listen.

I will recount some of these acts to you:

1. When my wife whom I loved died, I did not cry. I learned that when the enemy comes and humiliates leaders and peoples, that the people do not cry, being under severe shock of what had befallen them.

2. I shaved my head and placed my hair in three piles:

The First Pile: I burned with fire, for the enemy will burn Jerusalem.

The Second Pile: I cut with the sword, for many will perish by the sword.

The Third Pile: I threw up in the air, for many will be taken and will be scattered in a faraway land.

When the soldiers arrested me and took me to Babylon (Iraq), I prophesied that they will return and will burn the city of God. I also prophesied that the Jews will return from Babylon and will rebuild Jerusalem.

Such behavior of mine helped the people remember their message long after I died. Furthermore, the Jews learned that they must obey God.

Question: Why did God allow Ezekiel to act out some messages?

Tobit and His Son
Tobit 1–4

I am Tobit. I will tell you my story. I used to live in Samaria.

God was very patient with Israel and its kings for many generations. At some point, He allowed for the Assyrians, who worship idols, to defeat His people. They took many Jews captives to faraway land, and brought foreigners to live in Samaria along with the few Jews whom they left there. Throughout the years, the Jews and foreigners married each other, which caused the inhabitants of the kingdom to become a blend of Judaism and paganism, called Samaritans. A great enmity developed between the Samaritans and the Jews.

I was among the ones taken captive by the Assyrians to Nineveh.

I loved God and consecrated all my life to serve my brethren, those in need. Even though I was away in captivity, I never stopped loving the Lord; I did all that was in my power daily to serve my brethren—the captives.

I had a son named Tobias, and he, too, loved God.

God gave me grace in the eyes of the king. He liked me and granted me liberty to travel. I was able to feed the hungry, clothe the naked, and bury the dead.

One day, I returned home tired, after I buried the dead, and slept by a wall which had a bird's nest in it. Alas, some of bird droppings fell on my eyes, and I became blind. I never doubted God's love for me. I always thanked Him instead, despite the mocking of my wife and relatives because of my situation.

When I felt that my time to die was fast approaching, I summoned Tobias, my son, and bade him my farewell words of wisdom.

I commended him to honor his mother all the days of his life, to love God, never consent to sin, give alms to the poor, live a life of purity, be humble, not delay settling laborers' pay, do to others what he would like others to do to him, ask for the counsel of wise men, and for God to bless him all the days of his life.

I asked him to go see a friend of mine in Medes, named Gabael, give him a note, and get a large amount of silver, which he had borrowed from me.

Tobias and Archangel Raphael
Tobit 5–14

I am Tobias. I promised my father, Tobit, to do as he had commended me. I met a young man who seemed to be ready to embark on a journey. I did not know that he was really Archangel Raphael. I asked him to guide me to the way that leads to the region of the Medes. He replied saying that he was going to the same town and to the same person whom my father had asked me to see, and that he would be traveling with me on my journey.

I began the journey and was followed by my dog. I lodged by the Tigris River on the first day. I wanted to wash my feet. All of a sudden, a monstrous fish came up to devour me. But, the Archangel Raphael saved me from it, and asked me to keep the heart of the fish, its gall, and its liver.

I asked my friend, the angel, saying, "Where would you like us to sleep tonight?" He suggested this to me, "There is a man named Raguel, a near kinsman of your tribe, and he has a beautiful daughter named Sarah." Every time she gets married, her husband dies. So the angel recommended that I be not be afraid to marry Sarah, He asked me to burn the fish's liver on the coal. I listened to him and married Sarah. We prayed for three days.

I heeded all that my friend, Archangel Raphael told me to do, and he went to see Gabael at my request, and brought the money.

I decided to return to my father, but Raguel asked me to stay. I told him that my father and mother must be worried because I was supposed to have returned sooner. I insisted that I leave right away and return home. Thus, Raguel gave me his daughter, Sarah, and half of all his possessions of cattle, cows, and a lot of silver. He bade us farewell in joy and peace.

I returned to my father, along with my friend. There, I placed the gall of the fish on my father's eyes and prayed. God allowed him to see again.

My family thanked my friend for what he had done with me. As for him, he asked that we give thanks and praises to God, and told us that he is Archangel Raphael, who stands before the Lord. We were filled both with fear and inner peace at the same time when we heard this. All of a sudden, he disappeared while saying to us, "Peace be with you." Thus, we thanked God for His care for us.

It is Good That We Complain to God!
Habakkuk 1

I am the prophet, Habakkuk. I wish to whisper in your ear, "It is alright to complain to God." Even those who love Him complain to Him.

I was very sad. I know it is a weakness that I have. I was very distressed. I found that there were more wicked people than righteous ones.

I spoke with God to convey my grievance to Him, saying, "Why do you stay quiet, O Lord, for the wicked keep on harming the righteous."

God replied and said, "I will send the Chaldean army to punish them. Wait, and you shall see the destruction which will befall Jerusalem and My temple."

So, I said, "But the Chaldeans are more wicked than the most wicked of Your people! Why would You send them to punish those who are better than they?"

To which God replied, "Trust Me. For the punishment of My people at the hands of the Chaldeans will lead many to return to Me and repent. And I will take them in My bosom. For I love My people. I will then go on punishing the Chaldeans, because they rejoice over My people. But I will take back the ones who repent and return to Me. I love all mankind."

I learned that God's wrath is mercy and love. I sang saying, "O Lord, I love Your work in the midst of the years…. In wrath remember mercy."

In the Palace of a Pagan King
Daniel 1

I am Daniel.

I was a prince in the royal palace in Jerusalem. In the third year of the reign of King Jehoiakim, the king of Judah, the army of Nebuchadnezzar came from Babylon (Iraq). They attacked Judah and detained the members of the royal family and the nobles. I was among them, along with my three friends—the three youths—Hananiah, Azariah, and Mishael. They took me to Babylon and I was very sad. This was because of the iniquities of our people.

The king ordered that we learn the language of the Chaldeans at his expense.

I decided in my heart to remain faithful to my God, even if I was denied access to the Temple and Jerusalem, and to the city of God.

My God granted His grace to my three friends and I. We declined to eat of the king's food, for it was of the idols' sacrifice. In spite of this, God gave us splendor of body, and granted us gifts and wisdom. He also granted me the ability to interpret visions and dreams.

The king always boasted of our handsome appearances, as well as our knowledge and wisdom, of which God had bestowed upon us.

A Fiery Furnace, or the Presence of God?
Daniel 1–3

One more time, I am Daniel, reporting from Babylon.

With the help of God, I was able to interpret two strange dreams to King Nebuchadnezzar. One of the dreams led him to destroy the clever men and magicians, for they did not know how to interpret it. God revealed the dreams to me and provided me with their interpretations.

I was appointed to be the king's adviser. He consulted with me for every big and small matter, and the Lord provided me with the answer. God also granted favor in the eyes of the king to my friends, the three youths.

The king believed he was a god, forcing people to prostrate to him and worship him. Thus, the king ordered his people to erect a huge golden statute in his likeness, and ordered everyone to fall down and worship the statue. My three friends, Hananiah, Azariah, and Mishael, refused to do so, saying, "We only worship God, our God, regardless of what the king does to us." Some people went and told the king that they refused to worship the golden statue, and so the king ordered that they be thrown in the fiery furnace. When they were in the furnace, the king saw a fourth Person with them, looking very bright. That was the Word of God! He came to guard them to safety, so that the fire does not harm them in any way. Not even one hair on their body was singed!

Question: Why did the fire not harm the three youths?

A Feast Destroys the Kingdom of Babylon
Daniel 5

For a third time, I am Daniel. King Belshazzar made a great feast, and invited a thousand of his lords. They drank a lot of alcohol and were mocking the living God. The king gave a command to bring the holy vessels, which his father Nebuchadnezzar had taken from the temple in Jerusalem. Everyone began to use them to get drunk.

All of a sudden, the fingers of a man's hand appeared and wrote incomprehensible words. Then the king was greatly afraid and began trembling. Thus, he ordered that they bring him whoever can read and interpret these words to him, so that he would give them many valuable gifts. They could find no one able to do so!

Finally, his mother, the queen, came and told him about me, for I had revealed and interpreted his father's dreams. Then he called for me immediately and offered a reward if I interpreted the writings. I answered and said, "Let your gifts be for yourself, and give your rewards to another, Belshazzar. You have lifted yourself up against the Lord of heaven. This is the reason He sent what was written. And this is the interpretation: God has ended your life and your kingdom. You have been weighed, and found wanting. Your kingdom has been divided, and given to the Medes and Persians."

Then the king gave the command, and they clothed me with a royal outfit and put a chain of gold around my neck. That very night, the Medes and Persian enemies seized Babylon. Thus, Belshazzar's kingdom came to an end, and the Babylonian Empire was totally annihilated.

An Angel in the Den of Lions
Daniel 6

Again, I am Daniel. The king of the Medes and Persians changed the government of Babylon, and divided the kingdom into one hundred and twenty divisions to be ruled by a governor, and appointed a governor to each one. Then he chose me and two other ministers to oversee these governors. God granted me much more success than the other two. They felt that I had become very close to the king, and suspected that I would be made their superior and the second in command after the king.

So the ministers, governors, and palace workers were jealous of me, and sought to find some charge against me concerning the kingdom, but they could find no charge or fault. Finally, these men said, "The only way to get rid of him is through his relation with his God that he worships in all faithfulness. You know full well that he enters his room and prays to his God three times a day."

Thus, they said to the king, "O King Darius, may you live forever! We are aware of how great you are! We have consulted together that your highness make a firm decree that no one could petition anything from any god or man, except you, O king. And whoever breaks this decree shall be cast into the den of lions. Now, O king, establish the decree and sign the writing, so that it cannot be changed!"

The king issued the decree that everyone must kneel down and petition him when they are in need of anything. I was only prostrating before God, and praying to Him only.

Some evil people told the king that Daniel is still praying to God, and not to you. Thus, the king commanded that I be thrown in a den of hungry lions!

God sent His angel and shut the lions' mouths, so that they did not touch me nor devoured me, but were playing with me. I was safe the whole night!

Question: What is the reason the lions did not eat Daniel?

Bel the Idol
Daniel 14:1–21

I am Daniel. When Cyrus, the Persian, was crowned king of Babylon, God gave me grace in his eyes, and so, he honored me and placed me in a position higher than his own friends.

The Babylonians had an idol called Bel. One day, the king asked me why I do not worship the statue. I answered him saying, "I do not worship a statue made by men, I worship the living God."

The king said to me, "Do you not believe that Bel is alive? Do you not see him eat and drink every day?"

I smiled and told the king, "Do not be deceived, O king. He does not eat!"

I asked the king to send all the seventy Bel priests out along with their wives and children, then place the food and wine on the altar, shut the door, and have it sealed with the king's ring. I also asked my servants to spread little ashes all over the temple in the presence of the king only. Then, the king and I went there early the next morning, and when the doors were opened, the king looked at the table and did not find the food; and so he exclaimed, "How great is Bel!"

I smiled as usual, and held the king so that he does not go in. I asked him to look on the floor. There, he saw footsteps of men, women, and children.

The king got angry, interrogated the priests and their families, and they showed him the hidden doors that they use to enter into the temple, and eat whatever was on the table. Therefore, the king put them to death and destroyed the statue and the temple!

187

A Huge Dragon, or a God?
Daniel 14:22–42

I am Daniel. I will tell you a story that will make you very sad.

I used to enter my room in Babylon and weep for the people of Babylon that did not worship their Creator. They worshipped a huge serpent (dragon) instead of God.

The king said to me, "You were saying that Bel the statue was just a piece of solid bronze. What do you think of the great dragon god?"

I answered the king, saying, "Do you believe that he is a living god that does not die? Please allow me to kill him without using any weapon."

Thus, the king allowed me, and I brought a pitch and fat and hair, and boiled them together. I made lumps and gave it to the dragon. The dragon ate it and died.

The Babylonians gathered against the king and asked him to deliver me to them. They carried me and threw me in a den that had seven hungry lions, and left me there for one week.

My God sent the prophet Habakkuk to me in the den. He brought me food. I ate, and the angel returned Habakkuk to his place.

Seven days later, the king came to look at the den. There he found me sitting in the midst of the lions. The king cried out with a loud voice, saying, "Great are you, O Lord, the God of Daniel!"

The king drew me out of the den and proclaimed, "Let all the inhabitants of the whole earth worship the God of Daniel; for He is the Savior, working signs, and wonders."

189

Returning to Jerusalem
Haggai

After Judah's captivity in Babylon, both peoples, Israel and Judah, got together as one Jewish nation. God did not forsake them, but sent them prophets to guide them. He also sent them Queen Esther to save them, and the three saintly youth.

Seventy years had passed when Cyrus issued a decree allowing the Jews, who so wish, to return to Jerusalem and rebuild their temple.

When the elders saw the new building, they remembered the greatness of Solomon's temple, and began to weep.

God sent me to them. I told them that the new temple is greater, not in its architecture or its splendid furnishing, but because Christ the Lord, whom we expect, will come and enter it, erecting a new and greater temple, which is the Church of the New Testament.

Another Old Testament prophet came to assert that Christ the Lord, the Sun of Righteousness, would shine upon the world.

An Orphan Girl Becomes a Queen
Esther 2

I am Esther. I will tell you my story.

Persia (the area of Iraq and Iran today) was the greatest empire. The Persian King Ahasuerus divorced his wife, Vashti, and desired to have another wife to be made queen in her place.

His palace staff advised him to bring the most beautiful girls in the kingdom to live in the palace, be nourished with special food, and be fragranced with the finest scents that would be spread on their bodies for an entire year.

The king liked this advice; so, and they gathered the most beautiful girls. I was among them, for I obeyed my cousin. I am a Jewish orphan girl, raised by my cousin Mordechai. I listened to him and obeyed him.

One year later, the king met all the girls, fell in love with me, and made me queen. Then, the king made a great feast—a huge banquet—offered valuable gifts, and honored me before all his officials and nobles. But, I did not care about the palace, the riches, and the honors I got from all the people.

Do you know?

The royal palace assigned seven girls to attend to every girl for an entire year? For you, God sent you His Holy Spirit that dwells in you in the Holy Mystery of the Myron (Confirmation or Christmation). Thus, your spirit was made very beautiful, and all the heavenly creatures, waiting for the day of the Lord, welcome you, and you acquire a great glory!

Esther Saves Her People
Esther 3–10

I am Mordechai. I want to tell you my story with the arrogant Haman.

King Ahasuerus, king of Persia, chose an arrogant, proud man, named Haman, to assist him with all the matters of the kingdom, which extended from India to Turkey. Everyone who would run into him in the palace had to bow to him. I refused to do so. When Haman found out that I was a Jew, he told the king that my people do not obey the laws. Thus, the king issued a decree to kill all the Jews in the whole kingdom on the same day.

Esther asked that I and all the people I know to fast, so that God may grant her favor in the eyes of the king. She, too, fasted, prayed, and humbled herself before God. She invited the king and Haman to a feast that she prepared for them.

The king lost sleep that night and asked his servants to bring him his book of the records of the chronicles. He was surprised to find that I had saved him from a plot to kill him.

In the morning, the king asked Haman, "What shall be done for the man whom the king delights to honor?" Haman thought that the king was referring to him, so he told him that this person should ride on the king's horse, wear royal garments, a royal crest be placed on his head, and proclaimed, "Thus shall it be done to the man whom the king delights to honor!" Then, the king said to Haman to do so with me. Haman became very angry, but had no choice except to do as the king had ordered.

Queen Esther had her banquet. The king asked her about her petition. She told him that all her people would be killed the same day. The king became angry as he learned that this was because of Haman, and left.

Haman fell down at Esther's feet, pleading that she saves him. Then, the king entered and ordered him to be killed at once. Therefore, they brought the cross, which was prepared for me to be crucified on it, and crucified him instead of me. That day became a holiday that the Jews celebrate every year. It is called the "Feast of Purim."

Question:
Why does God allow tribulations to befall us?

Ezra, the Scribe and Priest
Ezra 6

I am Ezra. I am a priest and scribe. I love the word of God. I gathered all the books of the Old Testament, and I was careful to obey the Law.

Cyrus, the founder of the Persian Kingdom, and the victor over Babylon, declared that Jews who wished to return to their homeland were allowed to do so. We were allowed to rebuild the temple. He returned the temple's vessels to them, which the Babylonians had stolen.

The people of God rebuilt the temple, which the enemy had destroyed.

The construction stopped until Artaxerexes, king of Persia, came to power. He sent me, and I came to Jerusalem with another group of captive Jews.

The people labored hard to finish the construction of the house of the Lord and to pray. They were pleased because God rejoices when we bow down and pray to Him in His house. We, too, are happy with Him.

Question:

Do you remember to pray in your room and in church?

Nehemiah
Nehemiah 3–12

I am Nehemiah. I was the king's cupbearer in the king's palace in Babylon. The cupbearer had to be happy and cheerful when he gave the king a drink. He made me governor of Jerusalem. I loved God and was courageous. I feared no one, for God was with me. God helped me to rebuild the souls with the faith. This is my story.

One day, one of my brethren, Hanani came with men from Judah. I asked him about Jerusalem, the city of my fathers. He told me that its walls were broken and its doors were burnt. I was very sad. I prayed and fasted.

I gave the king wine to drink; and he asked me, "Why are you sad, Nehemiah?"

I said "I am sad because of my city, Jerusalem, which contains the tombs of my fathers."

He replied, "What is your petition, Nehemiah?"

I prayed quickly to God in heaven before I replied to the king, so that God may speak through my mouth, and said, "I would like you to send me to Judah, to the city of the tombs of my fathers to rebuild it." The king agreed. I went there, met the people, and told them, "Come and let us build the wall of Jerusalem, that we may no longer be a reproach."

When my enemies laughed at me and mocked the construction and the walls that I was building, I told them, "The God of heaven will grant us success, for we are His servants; let us rise and build." I began to build the wall, but some evil people resisted. So I divided the people into two groups: one to build the wall, and the other to guard the city. The people who built the wall carried their weapons, ready for any sudden attack from the enemies of God.

We finished rebuilding the wall in fifty-two days. Ezra, the scribe, came and read the Book of the Law before the entire people. All the people were happy that the wall was built. **Question:** Do you pray before you begin any work?

The Maccabees
1 and 2 Maccabees

I am King Antiochus Epiphanes. I did not like the Jews—God's people. I was doing all that was in my power to force the Jews to leave their faith and traditions. I persecuted whoever believed in the living God.

I ordered idol worship in the temple, along with the worship of God. Later on, I sent letters to Jerusalem, declaring the following:

1. Stop sacrifices and burnt offerings in the temple.
2. Do not keep the Sabbath or celebrate Jewish holidays.
3. Defile the temple and sacred places with the slaughtering of pigs and unclean animals.
4. Build altars, houses, and temples for the idols.
5. No circumcision of children is allowed.
6. Do not follow the Laws of Moses.

The Maccabees endured much because of my behavior. Some loyal and faithful people to God had to hide in shelters, because they feared me.

Mattathias, the Priest
1 and 2 Maccabees

I am Mattathias, the priest. I was distressed at the suffering of my people, the defiling of the holy city, and the harsh behavior of Antiochus Epiphanes. I prayed, saying, "Alas that I should have been born to witness the ruin of my people and the ruin of the Holy City, and to sit by while she is delivered over to her enemies."

The king asked to see me to tell me and my sons nice things, and to ask us to obey him, so we would be friends with him. He also gave us many gifts.

I answered the king plainly, saying, "Even if every nation living in the king's dominions obeys you, I, my sons, and my family will not obey you, and will not worship idols, and will still follow the Law of God!"

I spoke with my brethren, the Jews, and said, "Let everyone who has any zeal for the Law, the word of God, come out and follow me."

Then, I fled with my sons into the hills, and all those who loved the Law of the Lord surrounded us.

My son, Judas Maccabaeus, was courageous and strong. He organized an army.

Question: Do you love the word of God, memorize it, and observe it?

Judas Maccabaeus
1 and 2 Maccabees

I am Judas Maccabaeus. My father, Mattathias, died in 146 B.C. All the people of Israel were sad.

I mounted an army, and was aided by all my brothers; all those who followed me happily went to battle with me.

Antiochus Epiphanes sent a great, huge, and strong army against me. Those who followed me said, "How can we, being a small number and weak because of fasting, stand up and face such a large and strong crowd?"

I assured them that God saves whether we are many or few. Victory is not because of a great number, but by heavenly power.

Indeed, through the help of God, we defeated the leaders whom Antiochus Epiphanes sent. My men regained Jerusalem and our temple, and destroyed the pagan temples. They asked the Lord to not punish them by handing them over to evil and blasphemous people.

Antiochus Epiphanes rode his chariot in arrogance and pride, in high speed, without stopping, until he reached the place where Jews were buried together in a common burial place. All of a sudden, in his speed and haste, he fell off the chariot, and suffered excessive wounds. As he became very weak, he prayed to the Lord, and promised to redeem himself, fixing all the evils that he had done in the past. But, after a few days, when he was found unfaithful and dishonest, many left him, and he died enduring bitter pains.

Question: How do you defeat sin?

The Martyrdom of Eleazar
2 Maccabees 6

Welcome! I am an old man who loves God. I am ninety years old. I used to live during the period between the return of the Jews to their land until the coming of Christ the Lord. We lived under the occupation, and the rule of foreign forces: one time, under the rule of the Persians, another time under the Macedonians, and a third time, under Egypt. Also, we were under the rule of Syria and Rome, too.

During the rule of the Syrians, Antiochus Epiphanes dealt with us violently. He forced us to worship statues, to sacrifice to idols, and to desecrate the Sabbath. Many of us preferred to be martyred rather than to heed this king's orders.

I was asked to eat meat that the Law forbids that we eat. I refused and preferred to listen to God's command.

Some told me to fake eating it to save my life, but I refused; because of that, many youth did not like me. I suffered much pain.

Prayer:

O Lord, teach me to obey Your word, and not fear those who force me to violate Your commands.

The Martyrdom of a Mother and Her Seven Children
2 Maccabees 7

I am a mother. I had seven children. King Antiochus Epiphanes arrested my children and I.

He tortured us so that we would eat pork and violate the Law. My older son tolerated the cutting of his tongue, for he insisted that he would not violate the divine Law.

My children endured much pain and suffering. I encouraged them joyfully, until they received the crown of martyrdom.

Between The Maccabees and the Coming of Christ the Lord

After the death of Antiochus Epiphanes, his son labored to defeat the Jews. Nonetheless, the Maccabees defeated his large army by relying on God.

Finally, the Syrian king was forced to enter into a peace treaty with them. Judas made arrangements with the Romans, who promised him help and protection.

The Jews were split into two groups: Pharisees and Sadducees, and they had disagreements between them on who should be the leader. The Romans took advantage of the situation, by pretending to bring about peace in Judah, and then, occupied it. They also appointed a foreign king named Herod.

This way, the Jews lost their freedom until Christ the Lord came.

Judah was not the only one waiting for Him, but the whole world was expecting the arrival of the Savior.

Sin increased tremendously and iniquity ruled the world. Everyone was in need of the advent of the Savior, our Lord Jesus Christ from heaven, to proclaim the truth and save and bless mankind.

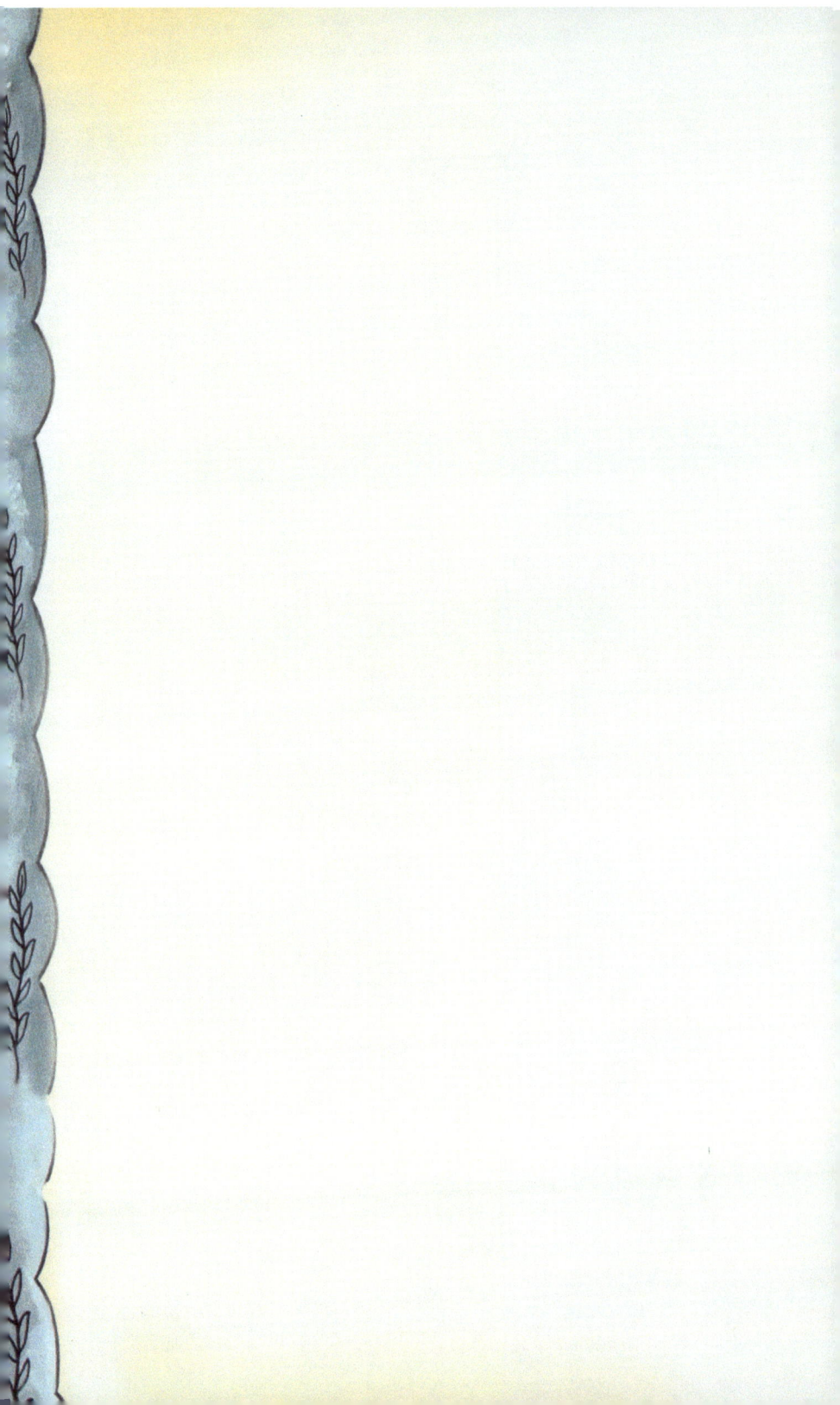

www.ingramcontent.com/pod-product-compliance
Lightning Source LLC
Chambersburg PA
CBHW040455240426
43663CB00033B/2